Inhabiting the Promised Land

Exploring the complex relationship
between archaeology and Ancient Israel
as depicted in the Bible

Margreet L. Steiner

OXBOW | books
Oxford & Philadelphia

Published in the United Kingdom in 2019 by
OXBOW BOOKS
The Old Music Hall, 106–108 Cowley Road, Oxford, OX4 1JE

and in the United States by
OXBOW BOOKS
1950 Lawrence Road, Havertown, PA 19083

This book is a translation of *Op zoek naar... De gecompliceerde relatie tussen archeologie en de Bijbel*
© Margreet L. Steiner 2015

Paperback Edition: ISBN 978-1-78925-330-6
Digital Edition: ISBN 978-1-78925-331-3 (epub)

A CIP record for this book is available from the British Library

Library of Congress Control Number: 2019945010

Printed in the United Kingdom by Short Run Press

Typeset in India for Casemate Publishing Services. www.casematepublishingservices.com

For a complete list of Oxbow titles, please contact:

UNITED KINGDOM
Oxbow Books
Telephone (01865) 241249
Email: oxbow@oxbowbooks.com
www.oxbowbooks.com

UNITED STATES OF AMERICA
Oxbow Books
Telephone (610) 853-9131, Fax (610) 853-9146
Email: queries@casemateacademic.com
www.casemateacademic.com/oxbow

Oxbow Books is part of the Casemate Group

Front cover: Photo by Margreet Steiner
Back cover: Photos by David Bivin

Contents

List of figures

Prologue

Almost every week headlines shout out that new archaeological discoveries have been made that confirm the biblical stories. The palace of David has been discovered, an inscription mentioning Goliath, the signet ring of queen Jezebel, a text about the prophet Balaam. But how correct are these stories? Is it really possible to connect unequivocally Bible and archaeological findings? This book tries to provide an answer.

For many people it is clear: the actions and beliefs of Ancient Israel are described in the Bible. The stories about its peoples and kings, struggles and wars, deities and shrines, are supposed to have been told and retold throughout the ages and recorded in ancient archives. At a certain moment in time these stories have been assembled in the Bible. They are history.

This, however, is a simplified version of what modern scientific research has unearthed. From the 19th century onwards, if not before, scholars have doubted the historical reliability of many biblical stories and archaeological research has hardly been able to confirm their historicity. But the critical comments of modern scientific research are hardly noticed by the general public; these comments drown in the sea of websites and books maintaining that archaeological findings confirm the biblical narrative and that 'the Bible is history'.

The aim of this book is to fill this lacuna and to describe the often complicated relationship between archaeology and the Bible. It focuses on the information that archaeology can provide on the lives and beliefs of the ancient peoples that once inhabited the land in which the Bible was written and on the question of how this information relates to the biblical stories. It does not give a comprehensive account of all that archaeology has to offer but rather aims at providing some examples of how the interplay of archaeology and biblical stories works and how to interpret the discrepancy that may exist between the results of archaeological research and the biblical narrative. It thus offers an introduction into the field from the standpoint of an archaeologist.

All this is work in progress. New finds and new research methods may change the archaeological picture, while modern biblical research provides ever more insight in how and when the Bible was composed. This book is the result of my personal experiences as an archaeologist and a teacher, of the comments made by my students, and the fun we had when we went over countless biblical texts and archaeological articles. It is written for whoever delights in investigating complicated questions – unabashed and with an inquisitive mind.

Chapter 1

In search of ... archaeology and the Bible

This is a book about the relationship of archaeological finds and biblical texts. It examines what we really know of the region in which Ancient Israel as depicted in the Bible emerged, and what aspects of the biblical narrative can be linked to the historical framework drafted by archaeological research.

This introductory chapter will provide a short overview of what archaeology is and what it does and will look at the differences between 'biblical archaeology' and 'archaeology of the Levant'. Excavated inscriptions, too, need to be analysed; their content cannot be taken for granted. Then the issues surrounding the history of the Bible as a book will be discussed: which historical material does it contain and when was that written down? A short overview of the chronology of the region is presented in the last section.

Of course these paragraphs can only touch upon the subjects discussed. For more information the reader is referred to the *Further reading* section at the end of the book.

Terminology

The *Ancient Near East* is the geographical region in which the old civilizations from Mesopotamia to Egypt to Turkey (Anatolia) flourished (Fig. 1.1). It is a much-used term in scholarly circles. Many universities offer courses on 'Languages and cultures of the Ancient Near East' or 'Archaeology of the Ancient Near East'.

The *Middle East* refers to more-or-less the same region in modern times. Usually it does not include Egypt and Turkey.

Ancient Israel is the Israel as depicted in the Bible, where it is used to designate both the region and the people.

Palestine is a multi-faceted name. In Roman times, it was the name of the province that was located in today's Israel. After World War I it became the name of region under the British Mandate, which included the areas west of the river Jordan

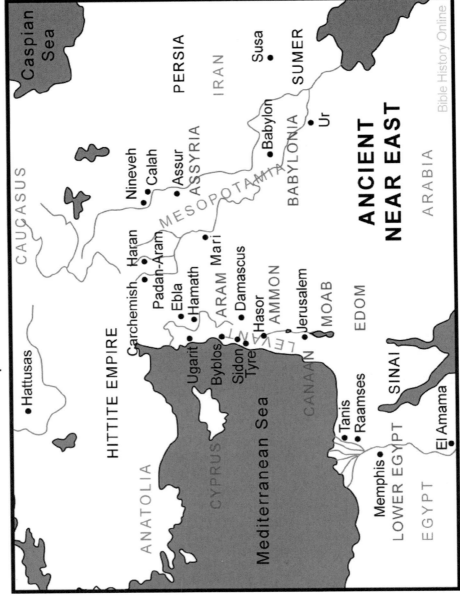

Figure 1.1 Map of the Ancient Near East (freely distributed from https://www.bible-history.com/geography/maps/map_ancient_near_east.html).

(Cisjordan) and that east of the river (Transjordan) (Fig. 1.2). When the Emirate of Transjordan was established in 1921, the name Palestine was used exclusively for Cisjordan. Lately it has become a general designation for the whole region, in order to avoid the names of the modern states of Israel and Jordan: Palestinian archaeology or the Archaeology of Palestine was a common term in university circles. Today the name Palestine is used for the Palestinian Authority and the (future) state of Palestine.

The *Levant* is the region stretching from northern Syria to southern Israel, and it includes the modern states of Israel, Jordan, the Palestinian Territories (together the Southern Levant), and Lebanon and Syria (Northern Levant) (Fig. 1.3). Strictly speaking the Bible originated in the Southern Levant, but to keep things simple, in this book the name Levant will be used.

The term *Bible* is used for the Jewish Bible, which in Christian tradition is called the Old Testament. For the translation of biblical texts the New International Version (NJV) is used.

Figure 1.2 The river Jordan near Jericho. This photo was made between 1898 and 1914 by the American Colony photographers (Matson Photographic Collection, public domain).

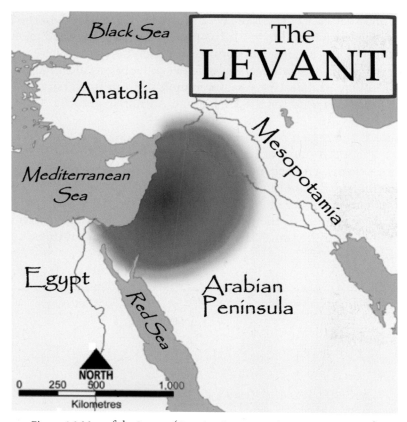

Figure 1.3 Map of the Levant (Creative Commons Licence CC BY-SA 3.0).

What is Archaeology?

Archaeology is not a technique, it is a science. A well-known and often used definition is:

> Modern archaeology is the scientific study of cultures (and technologies) from the past, with the aid of specially designed scientific methods and theoretical concepts.

If you think that is vague, you are right. But this definition highlights the fact that archaeology is the scientific study of ancient cultures. It is not just about excavating, even though it is sometimes presented as such. Excavations are simply a means to uncover the remains of those ancient cultures and preserve them for posterity (Fig. 1.4).

Many material remains are lost through natural causes (erosion, flooding), but even more through human action (digging, building, agriculture). In most western countries, excavation is only allowed on sites under threat from building activities. If a site is safe, it is left in peace. Things are different in the Middle East. There too the majority of sites is excavated because they are threatened by nature or humans, but pure scientific interest is still considered sufficient reason to get an excavation permit.

Figure 1.4 Excavations at Mudayna Thamad in 2008 (photo: Noor Mulder).

Of course, this scientific research is not done in a haphazard way (one would hope), but is always underpinned by scientific methods and concepts. As an archaeologist you have to adhere to certain scientific norms and values. For instance, you cannot select or publish only those facts or finds that support your theories, you have to be objective and show what goes against your ideas as well. And you must use scientific methods, both when digging and when you sit at your desk.

So, archaeology is more than just digging. It is the study of the remains of ancient cultures. This includes both excavated material and ancient texts. Those remains and texts need to be brought together in order to write the 'history' of a region.

Be aware: archaeology does not dig up those histories; archaeologists dig up artefacts such as stone walls, floor layers, pottery, glass, metal arrowheads, bread ovens and hearths. They find botanical residues, human remains, and animal bones which are sometimes made into artefacts such as needles. By studying and interpreting these finds they may be able to reconstruct the social, political and economic systems and the histories of the cultures they are researching.

Interpretation is an important but subjective filter. Every interpretation may have numerous alternatives, some of which are more likely than others. Paradigm shifts drag our interpretations and conclusions behind them. When the paradigm changes, then the interpretations change too. A scientific paradigm is a system of models and theories creating a framework for analysing and describing 'reality'.

Mudayna Thamad

As an example of archaeological research, I will use my own study of the pottery of Mudayna Thamad in Jordan. Mudayna Thamad is a small settlement in ancient Moab dating to the end of the Iron Age (see below). Excavations were conducted there from 1996 till 2012. I am studying the corpus of pottery sherds excavated in the years 1996–2004 (Fig. 1.5), whereby I focus on the following aspects:

Figure 1.5 Pottery from Mudayna Thamad (photo: Margreet Steiner).

1. The number of sherds of each functional type: how many cooking pots, jars, jugs, bowls, lamps, etc, were found and where were they found? In houses, on the street, in the gate? The distribution of these vessels over the site can tell me something about the use of the buildings and rooms. Some areas may have been kitchens, others reception or storage rooms.
2. How were the pots made? What forming techniques did the potters use, how did they decorate their vessels, what type of kiln did they use? These aspects give information on the technological level of the society.
3. What clays were used? Were all the pots made at or near the settlement from local clays? Or was there imported pottery too, made from non-local clays? And where did these imports come from? This gives clues about the economic relations of the site with other sites in the region or with other regions. Pottery may have been imported all the way from Greece or Assyria.
4. The distribution of pottery over the site may elucidate not only the use of space but also its social structure: did rich and poor quarters exist? Was there a particularly opulent building?
5. Dating the pottery securely places the site in the chronological history of the region.
6. The pottery may also tell something about the function of the site within the region and thus of the political structure of the society. Was it a farming village, fortress, town, or a palace complex?

7. How does the repertoire of finds compare to that of other sites? Sites in a border region or along the coast may have other pottery than sites more inland, as they have more contacts with other regions. This may give information of the inhabitants' world view and the exchange of ideas between regions.

These are some of the things that excavated pottery can shed light on. Of course, I also look at the combination with other find categories such as animal bones, bread ovens, stone tools, texts, or the spatial design of the building. Other archaeologists may focus in more detail on the technology of pottery production, or the designs in painted pots. Together, these pottery studies will end up as one chapter in the publication of the Mudayna Thamad Project.

Excavation is, therefore, a small, but very important part of archaeology. Studying and interpreting the excavated materials and their contexts are equally important, but take up much more time than the actual excavation. It has been calculated that just processing (that is documenting, drawing and photographing) the finds of a 3-month excavation takes at least 7 months. The research that follows and final interpretation may take many more years.

Biblical archaeology and archaeology of the Levant

Although both terms are used for what seems to be the same thing, there is actually a vast difference between biblical archaeology and the archaeology of the region from which the Bible originated: the Levant.

'Google' *biblical archaeology* and inevitably you will end up on Christian sites. Biblical archaeology is a term often applied in situations where archaeology is used to illustrate the biblical stories. Basically, this is a legitimate activity, but it has little to do with archaeology as a science. The term is also applied when archaeology is used to prove that 'the Bible is right'. This a hopeless exercise, as we shall see in the course of this book.

The most extreme form of biblical archaeology I found on a website that invited people: 'Welcome to dig the Bible!' By which it did not mean digging up old parchments! The idea behind this slogan is that the stories in the biblical texts can be easily verified by starting an excavation. The truth lies hidden in the ground and all we need is a spade and a trowel. Another such site claimed: 'Biblical archaeology examines archaeology and history as it applies to the Bible and helps in the defence of the Christian faith.' This turns archaeology into the servant of a religion.

Often a milder form of biblical archaeology is practised, whereby scholars assume that the biblical stories can be used as a historical source, albeit with some reserve, side by side with archaeology. Where these sources differ, a solution must be sought. In the following chapters we shall come across several examples of this procedure.

The latest offshoot is the use of archaeology by biblical scholars to *date* biblical texts. In the past this was not uncommon, but it was not done 'scientifically' – more a pick-and-choose exercise, using only those data fitting the purpose. Chapter 2 will present some examples of this.

The modern approach is more scientific. It starts with an objective framework of the period in question, based on archaeological data. The biblical text is then fitted into this framework, thus providing the context and date of the text. One example is the dissertation of Koert van Bekkum, a Dutch theologian. He questioned whether the events described in the Book of Joshua are a reflection of historical events. The written version is generally dated to the 7th or 5th century BC, just before or just after the inhabitants of Judah were sent into exile to Babylonia (more on this in Chapter 8), and it is considered largely fictional. Van Bekkum claims to have found indications for the historicity of some of the stories which, according to him, reflect a Late Bronze Age (13th or 12th century BC) society, rather than a 7th or 5th century one. However rigorous the scientific approach is in this example, archaeology is still used as the handmaiden of biblical studies. And that is, in essence, the defining characteristic of biblical archaeology.

Archaeology of the Levant is something else entirely. It is the archaeology of the region, regardless of biblical origins or stories. You can compare it to the archaeology of, for instance, the Low Countries or Great Britain, which presents an interpretation of (pre)history based on excavated remains. Archaeology of the Levant thus tries to unravel the history and prehistory of the region, based on archaeological research. Written sources, among which are some biblical texts, will then be incorporated at a later stage.

Often texts and archaeological finds do not 'add up'. Sometimes they complement each other, sometimes they contradict, and many times they do not connect at all. An example: Assyrian royal inscriptions detail the acts of the mighty kings, their building projects and military campaigns. They hardly ever mention the common people, who are living simple lives in the villages that provide the kings with food and labour. Archaeological research, on the other hand, focuses on the day-by-day activities of these common villagers and towns people. They built houses, grew barley, made pottery and metal tools, bought and sold materials, and were buried in simple graves. It is often difficult to connect these two sources as they refer to and give information on different aspects of a culture.

We need to keep in mind that the use of the Bible to interpret archaeological research, or the use of archaeology to enlighten biblical stories, has an extra handicap: the Bible is a not a *primary* written source. That means that the texts *as we have them* were mostly not written down in the period they describe. Compare this to the above-mentioned Assyrian annals glorifying the deeds of the mighty Assyrian kings. Even if the annals do no tell the truth or the whole truth (as is often the case), they were written down in the period in which those kings lived and acted. They are primary sources.

From the Bible we have only much later versions. We do not know when most of the biblical stories were put into writing, nor how truthfully they reflect the oral

Figure 1.6 Caves near Khirbet Qumran in which the Dead Sea scrolls have been discovered (Lux Moundi, Creative Commons Licence CC BY 2.0).

traditions at their roots. If a story was written down several centuries after the event recorded, how reliable is the story itself, the portrait of the landscape in which the story took place, or the customs described? Do they stem from the time referred to in the story, or from the time the story was written down?

And we do not even have the versions that were originally put into writing. The oldest written biblical fragments are the Dead Sea Scrolls dating from the 3rd–1st centuries BC (Fig. 1.6), and most codices of Bible books are medieval. That is much later than the supposed date of the stories described and also much later than the recording of these stories.

To be fair, the difference between these kinds of archaeology, biblical and archaeology of the Levant, is often somewhat blurred. Of course, biblical archaeology (in its less extreme form) is also interested in the region and it tries to be objective in its results; and of course archaeology of the Levant cannot ignore the Bible. The difference lies in the basic assumptions from which they start.

In the past, the archaeology of Israel and Jordan was mostly biblical archaeology. Nowadays most archaeologists do not work like that anymore, although it does creep in, occasionally. The problem these days lies mostly with biblical scholars who are using the results of archaeological research to illustrate or confirm the Bible. In theory, the gap between archaeology and biblical research should widen as times goes on, as each discipline asks different research questions and focuses increasingly on different subjects. However, somehow there are always people determined to squirm into this hole trying to close it. Biblical archaeology continues to flourish.

Inscriptions

Excavations in the Levant do not only unearth artefacts and structures. A growing number of interesting inscriptions have opened up new windows into the economic, religious and political circumstances of the Bronze and Iron Ages. They may also sometimes mention persons known from the Bible, such as King Mesha of Moab. A large stele mentioning his name was found in Moab, Jordan, glorifying his deeds and the support of his god Kemosh (see Chapter 7). He conquered the sons of Omri and liberated his country from Israelite occupation. Both kings, Mesha and Omri, are mentioned in the Bible. The excavations in Deir Alla in the Jordan valley in Jordan revealed a religious text which repeatedly mentions Balaam, son of Beor, a prophet who played a role in the biblical narrative around the Exodus and the Entry into the Holy Land by the Israelites (Chapter 9).

Another important corpus of short texts, written on storage jars and walls, was found in Kuntillet Ajrud in the Negev desert. These inscriptions invoke the god of Israel YHWH together with the Canaanite goddess Asherah, which caused quite a stir in the world of biblical scholarship (see Chapter 10). Sometimes Egyptian, Assyrian, Babylonian and Persian texts too provide information about events and people mentioned in the Bible.

Of course inscriptions, like other artefacts, need to be interpreted with reference to their context (where were they found, under what circumstances, together with what other artefacts, and how are they dated), as well as to their language and script, and their content. Often the context creates controversy among scholars, as does the content. Even the language of an inscription can be the subject of fiery debates. Take the Balaam text, mentioned above. According to most scholars it was written in an Aramaic dialect at the end of the 9th century BC. However, some maintain that the language is not Aramaic, but ancient Hebrew. For the interpretation of the text this matters quite a lot: was the region controlled by Aram or by Israel when it was written?

Texts, therefore, need to be treated with caution, just like other finds. The context is important, as is the connection with other texts found in the ancient Near East. More importantly, the content must not be accepted at face value. A king may tell us that he conquered a certain people but that does not mean that he actually did. Determining the *Sitz im Leben* (see Chapter 2) is vital for the understanding of a text: what was its purpose, who were the intended audience, under what the circumstances was it written? We will encounter these problems several times in the following chapters.

The Bible

About the Bible as a corpus of ancient texts, much more can be said than is possible here. For our subject – archaeology and ancient Israel in the Bible – the 'historical' books are the most important. These books recount the history of the People of Israel, from the day of the Creation to post-exilic times. The relevant books are (in order of the Jewish Bible):

- *The Torah*: the first five books, or Pentateuch in Greek: Genesis, Exodus, Numbers, Leviticus and Deuteronomy. These books comprise the story of the Israelites from the Creation to and including the Patriarchs (Genesis); the Exodus and the sojourn in the desert ending with the death of Moses (Exodus and Numbers); and God's laws and regulations (Numbers and Leviticus). The book of Deuteronomy is a repeat of these stories. Traditionally Moses is seen as the author of the Torah – writing under divine inspiration (Fig. 1.7).
- *The early Prophets*: Joshua, Judges, Samuel and Kings. These books describe the entry into the Promised Land (Joshua); the settlement in the land under the leadership of the judges (Judges); the rise of the kingdom and the split into the Northern kingdom of Israel and the Southern kingdom of Judah. Both nations are crushed a few centuries later by the Assyrians and Babylonians (Samuel and Kings). The authors of these books are, according to tradition, Joshua (the book of Joshua), Samuel (the books of Samuel and Judges), and the prophet Jeremiah (the books of Kings) (Fig. 1.8).
- *The historical books*: Chronicles, Ezra and Nehemiah. Chronicles retells the history of the People until the Exile, and Ezra and Nehemiah describe the return to the Land after the Exile. Traditionally these three books were considered to have been written by Ezra and Nehemiah, after the Exile.

The remaining books of the Bible are mostly non-historical and will not be dealt with here. The question of who wrote these Bible books, their dates, sources and purposes, are all subject to endless debate. For centuries it was taken for granted that Moses wrote the Torah and various prophets the other historical books. But eventually this consensus became unsatisfactory. In the 19th century the Bible became subject to scrutiny, not as a holy book, but as an ancient text, comparable to other ancient texts such as the classical historians and the Mesopotamian inscriptions that had just been discovered. All the questions above were asked: who, what, where, when, why and how. This is what is called the 'critical approach', not because it criticises the Bible, but because it looks at the Bible critically – critical here means doing objective research. There have been a number of critical approaches. I mention just two.

Redaction criticism

In the 19th century the German scholar Julius Wellhausen developed the *documentary hypothesis*. He had noticed (as had others before him) that the first five books of the Bible had different names for God: Elohim and YHWH (Jahweh). Therefore, he concluded, the written versions must have different sources: the E-source used the name Elohim, while in the J-source the name of the deity is YHWH. J would have been a Jahwistic document, originating in Judah in the 9th or 8th century BC, while E

Figure 1.7 Moses with the ten commandments by Rembrandt van Rijn (1659) (Germaldegalerie, Staatliche Museen, Berlin, public domain).

Figure 1.8 Icon of the prophet Jeremiah painted between 1700 and 1800. Exhibited at the Museum of Byzantine Culture, Thessaloniki, Greece. Made between 1700 and 1800 (public domain).

was a document from the northern kingdom of Israel, from *c*. 750 BC. These written sources would then have been edited by R (Redaktor or Editor) in the 7th or early 6th century BC in Judah, with traces of this editing still visible in the text. During the Exile, J and E would have merged with Deuteronomy (D). Deuteronomy was a separate document, with a strong emphasis on the rejection of other deities, and on the temple service in Jerusalem. The Priestly source (P), focusing on the role of the priests, was the latest addition.

Following Wellhausen, scholars discovered increasingly more sources, and eventually the picture became too complex to be workable. However, the original hypothesis, of the present books originating in different sources, and being edited several times, is still accepted, even though those sources are not as easy to distinguish as thought before.

Tradition critique

Another approach starts with the traditions embedded in the narratives. According to this approach the written versions have their origins in ancient oral and written traditions. Tradition critique seeks out these origins and the historical traditions that shaped the great narrative cycles. Gerhard von Rad and Martin Noth are important protagonists of this idea. Von Rad discerned three traditions in the earlier books: the desert tradition dealing with the Patriarchs, the Exile tradition and the Conquest tradition. These three eventually merged into the great narrative that runs from Genesis to Joshua. This approach is problematic in that it relies heavily on the idea of oral traditions which, by their very nature, cannot be verified.

There are many more hypotheses. Some claim that there is hardly any historical core to the biblical narrative – see Thomas Thompson's book *The Bible in History, How Writers Create a Past*. A book by Karel van der Toorn, entitled *Scribal Culture and the Making of the Hebrew Bible* claims that the Bible was composed by a group of professional scribes at the Jerusalem royal court, who repeatedly copied the stories, at the same time adapting them to the actual situation. Other hypotheses will be discussed in Chapter 2.

And now?

As already stated, all sources need to be interpreted. Archaeological finds, inscriptions and biblical texts – they are all 'mute' unless understood and translated by people. This is the great challenge for scholars as well as for the general public. How do we interpret the sources, from which perspective do we view and understand them, how do we bring them together?

Unsurprisingly, ideas about this vary widely, as do interpretations. In the following chapters we will take a critical look at biblical and extra-biblical sources relating to various persons, periods and buildings mentioned in the Bible, and at the different ways scholars have interpreted these sources.

Chronology

In this book I follow the chronology used in archaeology: that of the Bronze and Iron Ages. They are specified as follows:

Bronze Age
Early Bronze Age (3200–2400 BC)
Walled villages and towns, writing, international trade

Intermediate Period (2400–2000 BC)
Disappearance of the old towns, farming villages and large cemeteries

Middle Bronze Age (2000–1550 BC)
Renewed wave of urbanisation, large city-states

Late Bronze Age (1550–1200 BC)
Old towns deserted, and later reoccupied, Egyptian influence.

Iron Age
Early Iron Age (1200–1000 BC)
Philistines on the coast, new villages in the hill country

Late Iron Age (1000–587 BC)
The Age of the Kings – capitals are Jerusalem and Samaria
Increasing Assyrian influence from the 9th century onwards
Eventually the Assyrians subdue most kingdoms

Neo-Babylonian and Persian period (587–333 BC)
Many towns and cities destroyed, but later rebuilt
The Levant is part of the Neo-Babylonian and later the Persian empire

Chapter 2

In search of ... Abraham and his descendants

In this chapter we take a closer look at several biblical stories that deal with the history of the Israelite people: the stories on the patriarchs Abraham, Isaac and Jacob, the period of servitude in Egypt and the Exodus. These stories have played and still play a major role in the discussions over the historical reliability of the Bible. What exactly is the content of these stories, which aspects can be tested archaeologically, and what does that tell us?

We are dealing here with the 'great' narratives in the Bible, that reveal God's plan for the people of Israel. First there are the stories of the patriarchs – a family chosen by God, which became a whole people. The story begins with God's promise to Abraham that he will become a great nation, and the command to leave Mesopotamia (Fig. 2.1). In the period that follows it seems as if God has deserted his people – they become slaves in Egypt. But then Moses is told to break the bonds of servitude and lead his people out of Egypt. Disobedience to God's command (the golden calf episode) results in a 40-year sojourn in the desert, until the first generation has completely passed away. Only then are the people allowed to enter the land of Canaan – the land flowing with milk and honey. This 'history' is recorded in the first five books of the Bible, up to and including Deuteronomy.

These narratives reveal God's close interaction with His people, the promise of becoming a great nation and finding a new homeland, the troubles ensued, and the final fulfilment of the promise. These are the core narratives of the Bible, and many Jewish feasts have their roots heret: Pesach, Succoth and Shavuot (the feast of Weeks).

Abraham in space and time

Trying to place the patriarchs in real time and space immediately induces problems. Genesis 12–15 provides some clues as to the location of the narrative. First, there is the name of Abraham's home city: Ur of the Chaldees, and that of his destination: Haran. The name of Abraham's promised land is Canaan. Then there are the names of towns where he lived or passed through: Shechem, Gerar, Beersheba and Hebron. However, even a superficial look at these towns reveals that they flourished mostly in periods other than those in which the Abraham narrative can be placed.

Figure 2.1 Abraham caressing his son Isaac. Drawing by anonymous, after Rembrandt van Rijn. (Rijksmuseum Amsterdam, public domain).

The city of *Ur* is located in southern Mesopotamia and was excavated by Sir Leonard Woolley. The city flourished at the end of the 3rd millennium BC but was deserted after that period. In the 7th and 6th centuries BC, Ur was inhabited by the Chaldeans, who fought many fruitless wars against the Assyrians and the Babylonians. In the 6th century BC the Neo-Babylonian king Nebuchadnezzar (the conqueror of Jerusalem, who led the Judahites into exile), rebuilt the city on a grandiose scale. So, Ur of the Chaldees existed in the 7th and 6th centuries BC, just before and during the Exile. It cannot therefore have been Abraham's home city, because that story is dated long before the Exile.

Haran has the same problem. The town is identified with Harran in northern Syria which was an important trade centre both in the 3rd millennium BC and in the Neo-Babylonian period (7th and 6th century BC).

Canaan is the name of the land that God promised to Abraham: '... and they set out for the land of Canaan, and they arrived there. [...] The Lord appeared to Abram and said, To your offspring I will give this land. So he built an altar there to the Lord, who had appeared to him' (Genesis 12:5–7). There was a problem, though: 'At that time the Canaanites were in the land.'

Who were these Canaanites? In the Bible they are the original inhabitants of the Promised Land, but were they one people or several? Did they call themselves Canaanites? Were they a polity, a nation? What language did they speak? Does the name Canaanites exist outside the Bible? A closer look at the use of the name Canaanites, within and outside of the Bible, takes us to the Bronze Age and to the peoples that lived in the Levant at that time: the region that today includes Syria, Lebanon, Israel, Jordan and the Palestinian Territories.

In the Levant, the Bronze Age is the period from *c.* 3200–1200 BC. These two millennia saw development of the first towns, of writing and the first alphabet, and trade relations with Mesopotamia, Egypt, Anatolia and the Aegean. This was a flourishing region surrounded by Egypt in the south, Mesopotamia (Sumeria, Babylonia and Assyria) in the east, and Anatolia (the Hittites) in the north (see Figs 1.1 and 1.3).

Before returning to Abraham and his descendants, it is important to fill in the background onto which his narrative unfolds, namely Canaan and the Canaanites in the Bronze Age.

Canaanites in the Bible

The Bible mentions the Canaanite people 160 times, sometimes together with other peoples who supposedly inhabited the land that would later be called Palestine: Amorites, Hittites, Perizzites, Hivites and Jebusites (see for example Ex. 23:23). These are enigmatic texts that have received a lot of attention but sources beyond the Bible are silent about most of these peoples. Only the Amorites and Hittites are well-known

Bronze Age peoples, the others are unknown. We do not know whether they actually existed and if so, if they lived in 'the land of Canaan'.

The Canaanites are mentioned in the Bible several times as being the original inhabitants of Canaan, with whom the Israelites had to fight. The Joshua stories describe them as the inhabitants of the plains west of the hill country, where the Israelites lived (Philistines are not mentioned):

> The people of Joseph replied, The hill country is not enough for us, and all the Canaanites who live in the plain have chariots fitted with iron, both those in Beth Shan and its settlements and those in the Valley of Jezreel. But Joshua said to the tribes of Joseph, to Ephraim and Manasseh: You are numerous and very powerful. You will have not only one allotment but the forested hill country as well. Clear it, and its farthest limits will be yours; though the Canaanites have chariots fitted with iron and though they are strong, you can drive them out. (Joshua 17: 16–18)

Canaanites outside the Bible

Outside the Bible the names Canaan or Canaanites are seldom mentioned. An 18th century BC letter from Mari, the famous trade city on the Euphrates, speaks of 'thieves and Canaanites [ki-na-ah-nu] who make trouble in Rahisum'. It is unclear whether this refers to a specific tribe, a group of foreigners, or highwaymen.

The word Canaan is found on clay tablets from the 15th century BC city of Nuzi in Mesopotamia, where it refers to purple, the pigment made from murex shells along the coast ('in Canaan'). So the inhabitants of Canaan were named after the purple pigment in which they traded (unless it was the other way round, and the pigment purple (Canaan) was named after the people who extracted and sold it). The same thing happened centuries later, when the Greeks named the purple pigment 'phoenix' after the Phoenicians who traded in it.

An Egyptian stele from Pharaoh Amenhotep II, dated 1430 BC, refers to the coast of present-day Lebanon as 'the land of the Canaanites'. Some of the texts found in the Egyptian city of Amarna refer to 'the king of Canaan' (Ki-na-ah-hi).

None of these sources clarifies whether the word Canaan refers to a region, a city, a kingdom or, as some scholars believe, an Egyptian province. According to Niels Peter Lemche, the words Canaan and Canaanites are simply not clearly defined in the 2nd millennium BC. In his book *The Canaanites and their Land* he argues that the inhabitants of the alleged Canaanite territory did not know that they were Canaanites but considered themselves to be inhabitants of a tribe or city state.

Unsurprisingly, not everybody agrees with him. Most archaeologists and historians use the term Canaan loosely to designate the region between Egypt in the south, the harbour of Ugarit in the north, the Mediterranean in the west and the desert in the east; the inhabitants of this region they call Canaanites. So, except in the biblical sources (where it refers to the original inhabitants of the Promised Land), it is mostly a modern designation rather than a term commonly used in antiquity.

Archaeological research has shown that Canaan was not a nation but rather a collection of city-states, each controlling a certain territory. Its inhabitants were city-dwellers and farmers but also groups of nomads, who moved around to evade being ruled by any one of the cities. Throughout the Bronze Age the power of the cities fluctuated between strong and weak and at times it was even non-existent. In those periods most of the population was (semi)-nomadic.

Canaanite language and texts

'Canaanite' not only refers to the inhabitants of Canaan but also to the language they used. We do not know anything about spoken Canaanite but we do know about the written language as it appears on clay tablets, of which, fortunately, a large number have been found. The city of Mari, mentioned above, has yielded some 25,000 tablets, and the city of Ebla about 17,000.

In the Late Bronze Age, Ugarit was the most important harbour on the Canaanite coast. Thousands of clay tablets were found here, recording contracts, appointments, regulations, letters, myths and legends, sacrificial lists, and royal names. The texts were written in seven different languages, and five different scripts. The languages were Egyptian, Ugaritic, Akkadian, Cypriot, Babylonian, Hittite and Hurrite. Scripts used were syllabic and alphabetic cuneiform (explanation below), as well as Egyptian, Hittite and Cypro-Minoic hieroglyphs.

Ugaritic is a West Semitic language, closely related to Canaanite. It was written in an alphabetic cuneiform script (Fig. 2.2). Akkadian was the *lingua franca,* the language used in international contracts and correspondence. It used syllabic cuneiform script, like Babylonian and Hurritic. Hittites, Cypriots and Egyptians had their own language and script.

Language and script

In this context it is important to look briefly at the difference between language and script. You speak a language, you write a script. Any language can be written in any script – even a made-up script as children sometimes do – but certain scripts are better adapted to certain languages than to others. Take, for example, Turkish, the language most Turkish people speak. Turkish has never had a specially developed script. For a long time it used the Arabic script, while nowadays it uses the western, 'Latin' script. So I can read a Turkish newspaper, even out loud, because I know the script, but I do not have a clue what it says, because I do not know the language. Alternatively, if English is written in Arabic script, I cannot read it, even though I am fluent in English.

The earliest scripts, in the Middle East and elsewhere (Egypt, China), consisted of pictures (hieroglyphs). One donkey was depicted by a donkey, two donkeys by two donkeys, and for every extra donkey a line or a dot was added. A picture of a mouth meant 'mouth', an open mouth: 'speaking', a mouth with a cup: 'drinking' (Fig. 2.3).

Figure 2.2 Clay tablet from Ugarit in the Ugaritic language and alphabetic cuneiform script. It conveys a mythological poem from the Baal cycle and dates to the 14th century BC (Louvre Museum, Creative Commons Licence CC BY-SA 4.0).

Figure 2.3 Clay tablet with pre-cuneiform writings, from the end of the 4th millennium BC (Louvre Museum, public domain).

This system works well for administrative texts: 'the farmer (person) gives to the temple (building) two bags of grain (two bags)'. In whatever language you pronounce the pictures, the meaning remains the same.

However, this does not work for more complex texts, such as religious or political ones (agreements, hymns, legal texts) because of the very large number of pictures you would need to express them. The Chinese have followed the system through and ended up with over 40,000 pictorial signs. In the Near East the pictorial system developed into a syllabic one, in which each sign represents a syllable rather than a word. That reduced the number of signs, but it meant that an Akkadian text could no longer be read in another language, because the words differ. The syllabic signs developed into cuneiform script which means that the picture was simplified to a combination of wedges, pressed into the soft clay with a reed.

The next step, taken in the Near East but not in Egypt, was to reduce the meaning of a sign to a single sound – the birth of the alphabet. The oldest alphabetic inscriptions were found in Sinai, in the Egyptian copper mines where Canaanites worked, and date to the 16th century BC. This alphabet had 27 signs, all cnsnnts (I jest). It is called the Proto-Canaanite script. In the 14th century BC this idea was further developed in the large trade centre of Ugarit, using cuneiform signs (Fig. 2.2).

Still later a new alphabet was developed in Byblos. This script, originally developed by the Phoenicians in the 11th century BC, was adopted for Hebrew. In the 8th century BC the Greeks borrowed it from Phoenician traders. They developed it into the Greek alphabet, which formed the basis for the Latin alphabet which we use in this book (Fig. 2.4).

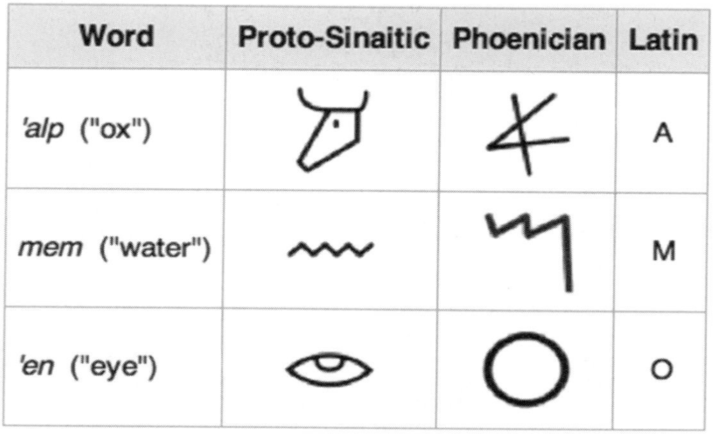

Word	Proto-Sinaitic	Phoenician	Latin
'alp ("ox")			A
mem ("water")			M
'en ("eye")			O

Figure 2.4 Development of the alphabet (Rozemarijn van L., Creative Commons Licence CC BY-SA 4.0).

Canaanite pantheon

The religion of the Canaanites is interesting by itself but also because Israelite religion (as presented in the Bible) is strongly influenced by Canaanite religion while fiercely condemning it at the same time. The Ugarit texts have opened a window into the Canaanite pantheon, modifying the very negative biblical account.

The main deity of the Canaanite pantheon is *El*, the Creator – ancient, wise and passive. He is often addressed as 'bull'.

His consort, *Athirat* or Asherah, the mother goddess, was commonly venerated in the shape of a tree. She is also called the 'Great Lady Athirat of the Sea'. Together El and Athirat have 70 children.

Baal, possibly one of El's sons (although he has also been named the son of Dagon) is the active, acting god. He is the weather god, god of thunder and lightning, and the war god. But he is also the god of the seasons, of growth and fertility (Fig. 2.5). The name Baal simply means 'lord'. One of the two temples on the acropolis of Ugarit was dedicated to Baal. According to the biblical accounts he later became the supreme deity of the Phoenicians.

Hadad was an important deity in the northern part of the Levant. A large temple dedicated to him was found in Aleppo, built in the Middle Bronze Age (*c.* 1800 BC), and in use until the end of the Iron Age (*c.* 700 BC).

Anat is Baal's sister, an important goddess of war and hunting.

Ashtarte or *Astarte* was Baal's consort, one of the lesser deities, and also responsible for war and hunting. She would later become the supreme deity of the Phoenicians, the goddess of love and fertility, which is how she is referred to in the Bible.

Dagon, a god of vegetation, has been described as the father of Baal, and may be identified with El. The second temple on Ugarit's acropolis was dedicated to him. The Bible mentions him as the supreme deity of the Philistines.

Many more gods feature in the texts of Ugarit, but those mentioned above are the ones that later became part of

Figure 2.5 Bronze statue of Baal from Ugarit. The raised arm originally held a spear or a lightning bolt (Louvre Museum, public domain).

the Phoenician pantheon and are mentioned in the Bible. Note that the Ugarit texts date from the Late Bronze Age, while the Biblical narratives describe what happened in the Iron Age and later. So it is interesting to see that the Iron Age Phoenicians adopted and venerated the Canaanite deities, even though some (such as Astarte) became more important, and others (such as El) less so.

YHWH is not mentioned in any Canaanite text and thus clearly not part of the Canaanite pantheon. It is thought that he originates in the southern Levant. El, the Canaanite supreme deity, has surprisingly been incorporated in the name 'Israel', which is thought to mean 'warrior/prince of God'; Jacob, after his struggle with the angel, was renamed Israel (Genesis 32:28). The god in that story listens to the name El, not YHWH. Perhaps YHWH and El were considered identical in certain periods.

Back to Abraham

A major point of discussion in the past, and still, is when the patriarchs lived. In other words, which historical period do they belong to? Whoever asks that question implicitly assumes that they actually *did* live in a certain period. That does not mean that every detail of their life stories has to be correct but it does imply that the stories, as handed down to us, have a historical core that survived in age-old oral traditions. By giving the patriarchs their rightful place in time, one can, as it were, 'prove' that the general story line – the nomadic patriarchs of the people of Israel, coming from elsewhere to the Promised Land – is historical. Of course, a drawback of this approach is that if you can *not* place the stories in a historical period, that would mean that they are not true. It is therefore vital for faithful researchers to find the 'correct' period for these stories.

This has become a parlour game with many dedicated players. The rules are as follows: details in the narrative that are historically or geographically verifiable are isolated and compared with historical data from the Bronze and Iron Ages – any earlier period is too early, any later one is too late. In this way one can arrive at the correct period and prove in one go that the stories are historical verifiable. There are various theories.

The patriarchs lived in the Intermediate Period (2400–2000 BC)

In the 1950s the archaeologist W. F. Albright dated the stories to the so-called Intermediate Period (2400–2000 BC). The preceding Early Bronze Age had seen growth of the first urban societies in Mesopotamia, Egypt and the Levant. This period would have ended with the invasion of the Amorites, a nomadic people from the Syrian steppe. According to the Bible the patriarchs were nomadic tent-dwellers. In this theory Abraham was a wealthy Amorite caravan trader, travelling from Mesopotamia (Ur) to Syria (Haran), and from there on to the south.

However, the hypothesis of an Amorite invasion destroying the urban civilization of the Early Bronze Age, has been discredited since. There are no traces of a major invasion in the region. The towns seem to have suffered a gradual decline, perhaps as a result of climate change (droughts). Also, archaeological evidence does not support the existence of a major nomadic people wandering over a wide geographical area. On the contrary, the Intermediate Period saw mainly rural societies, with farmers living in small and large villages. Moreover the towns, particularly those mentioned in the patriarchal narratives such as Hebron, Shechem, Bethel, Gerar and Beersheba, were unoccupied in the Intermediate period. So Albright's theory has little support left.

The patriarchs belong in the Middle Bronze Age (2000–1550 BC)

The cities mentioned in the patriarchal stories may not have been settled during the Intermediate Period, but they were certainly inhabited in the Middle Bronze Age. Researchers also found parallels between the patriarchal narratives and Mesopotamian legal texts such as those from Mari (17th century BC) and the Codex of Hammurabi (18th century BC).

The problem is that various prominent features of the Middle Bronze Age, such as the major fortified centres of Hazor and Megiddo, are missing from the patriarchal stories. In addition, the Mesopotamian parallels are not limited to the Middle Bronze Age, they appear in other periods as well. For example, in Nuzi (15th century BC) a barren woman was obliged to give a female slave to her husband to give birth in her place – as in the story of Sarah and Hagar. That puts a Middle Bronze Age setting of the stories in jeopardy – they may as well date to the Late Bronze Age, or even later.

The patriarchs date to the Early Iron Age (1200–1000 BC)

It has also been posited, based on things that were previously seen as anachronisms in the biblical texts, that the patriarchs lived in the Early Iron Age. Examples are the mention of the Philistine king of Gerar (Genesis 26:1) and the presence of Aramaeans (Genesis 25:20). Both peoples, Philistines and Aramaeans, have only been identified in the region in the Iron Age. But a setting of the patriarchal stories in the Early Iron Age would turn the biblical chronology completely on its head – after all, the consensus was that the people of Israel had fled out of Egypt and settled in the Promised Land in the beginning of the Early Iron Age. Everything that happened between Abraham and the Exodus would now have to be squeezed into a very short time frame. Apart from that, many details in the narratives are at odds with Early Iron Age society.

Conclusion

It has been suggested by, among others, Thomas Thompson in the 1970s, that the stories are not historical at all and therefore cannot be dated to a particular period. They are folk tales, possibly incorporating memories from ancient times – 'ancient' being a diffuse period with no particular time frame. That does not mean that the events themselves are completely 'made up' (we do not know that either) but we have to interpret the whole story cycle as a composition, put together with a particular purpose in mind and placed in an earlier period. That particular purpose is discussed below.

After Abraham

It is clear that if we are unable to place the patriarchal stories in a particular period this has consequences for the stories that follow it: the journey into Egypt, the enslavement and the Exodus. A quick overview of the stories will give an impression of the problems and possibilities.

Journey into Egypt

After Joseph had been sold to wandering Midianites and ended up in Egypt (Genesis 37), in Canaan things were going from bad to worse. There was a drought and Jacob and his family moved to Egypt, which still had corn they could buy. This was all thanks to Joseph, according to the Bible, although it is obvious that a country on the Nile would anyway suffer less from drought than a country dependent on rain.

Egypt, for the Canaanites, was not only a world power to which they were subjected regularly, but also a major trade partner and a refuge in times of need. An example of these trade relations can be found in a wall painting from a tomb in Beni Hassan, in Egypt, dated to *c.* 1900 BC. It shows a group of people, clearly not Egyptians, with their colourful dress and bearded men (Fig. 2.6). They wear sandals and leather boots, while donkeys carry their children and luggage. Their arms consist of bows and arrows, spears and a kind of boomerang. One of the men plays a lyre.

Figure 2.6 Line drawing of the scene of Asiatics in a tomb at Beni Hassan (Newberry, P. E., 1893, Beni Hasan I, pl. XXXI - https://digi.ub.uni-heidelberg.de/diglit/newberry1893bd1).

This group has been interpreted various: as musicians, as wandering blacksmiths, or as traders. According to the inscription they are 'Asians from the desert' (meaning nomads), bringing antimony. Antimony is a mineral found in the Sinai desert which is used in the preparation of make-up and medicines.

It will be clear that the biblical story of the journey into Egypt is indeed historical in the sense that journeys like these were common. However, there is no mention of a viceroy named Joseph in Egyptian annals and no clear historical setting for the story.

Sojourn in Egypt

Eventually, the Israelites were forced to work as slaves, building the cities of Pithom and Raämses (Exodus 1:11). These names could provide a clue. Raämses could be Pi-Ramesse, the 'house of Ramses' on the Nile, where Pharaoh Ramses II had a harbour town built in the 13th century BC, according to Egyptian annals.

However, whether Ramses II can be designated the pharaoh of the period of servitude remains to be seen. None of his inscriptions, nor those of his successors, mentions the events that form such an important part of the book of Exodus, such as the ten plagues, or the Exodus led by Moses. We may assume that, in general ,slaves and convicts did most of the hard work of building these cities and some of them could well have been Israelites who eventually fled the country. The story of a small group of fugitives, too small to be mentioned in the Egyptian annals, may well have become the core of a larger narrative, that of the exodus of a whole people.

There are various theories on the date of the Sojourn in Egypt and the Exodus, all focusing on the idea that linking the story to a specific period confirms the historicity of the story (our parlour game). Popular dates for the Exodus are 1570 BC, 1440 BC and 1240 BC.

Exodus in 1240 BC

The date of 1240 BC is preferred by most scholars. It fits a 13th century date for the Sojourn in Egypt, followed by the Exodus at the end of the 13th century. After a 40-year long Sojourn in the desert, the Conquest of Canaan then took place around 1200 BC. That coincides nicely with the archaeologically attested changes that signalled the transition from the Late Bronze to the Early Iron Age in and around Palestine. This thesis will be further explored in Chapter 3. However, we should remember that historical evidence for the Exodus is extremely meagre (see below). Trying to date a fictive event is always a tricky business.

Exodus in 1570 BC

The Sojourn of the Hebrews in Egypt has been (more commonly in older literature) connected with the Hyksos. They were a people with Semitic (rather than Egyptian) names who ruled northern Egypt for a while as the 15th dynasty but were expelled around 1570 BC. The Exodus is here interpreted as part of this expulsion. This date, however, creates problems for the biblical chronology, because it is very early; it would stretch the period of Judges to almost 600 years. There are simply not enough Judges mentioned in the Bible to fill that period.

Exodus in 1440 BC

This date takes its clue from 1 Kings 6:1 which says that the Exodus took place 480 years before the building of the temple of Solomon. The start of the building is commonly dated *c.* 966 BC by counting back from the Babylonian destruction of Jerusalem and then adding the reigns of the kings of Judah. Adding 480 to 966 gives 1446 BC. It would be difficult to find an archaeological underpinning of this date, which therefore is rarely attempted.

Dramatic events

The Exodus is accompanied by a series of dramatic events, such as:

- The revelation in the burning bush. This cannot be traced archaeologically.
- The ten plagues. There are no records of these in Egyptian sources.
- The crossing of the Red Sea. Pharaoh and his army perished in this event but there are no records of any of this in the Egyptian sources.
- The journey through Sinai to the Mountain of God, and the reception of the Ten Commandments. Scholars have spent many hours trying to trace the route of the Israelites but no archaeological clues have been found so far.
- The forging of the golden calf. This is an interesting story because bulls were venerated in Egypt and elsewhere as gods. However, no trace of this golden statue has been found.
- The 40-year Sojourn in the desert in the neighbourhood of Kadesh Barnea. This area has been subjected to extensive research, but no Late Bronze Age remains have been found. At the request of researchers I have studied the pottery from a large survey in the region. There were sherds from many periods but no remains from the Late Bronze (1550–1200 BC) or Early Iron Age (1200–1000 BC).
- The journey through Transjordan. According to the biblical narratives there were several large kingdoms and powerful cities in southern Transjordan. The Israelites had to negotiate or fight their way past them or make a large detour to avoid them. However, there is no archaeological evidence whatsoever for large cities in southern Transjordan in the Late Bronze or Early Iron Ages (the two possible dates for the Exodus).
- The presence of powerful cities in Canaan, seen by spies. There is hardly any evidence for large cities west of the Jordan either.

Scepticism

All in all there is little archaeological support for the biblical stories on the birth of the Israelite people. It is interesting to see that scepticism about the historicity of the biblical narratives follows the chronology of the narratives themselves. First there was doubt among 19th century scholars about the creation myths. Next the story of the Flood was wiped out – although there are still regularly 'scientific' expeditions which always seem to 'find' remains of Noah's Ark.

The stories about the patriarchs, the Sojourn in Egypt and the Exodus have been questioned since the middle of the 20th century and have been dealt with in this chapter. The stories regarding Israel's Entry into the Promised Land were heavily debated in the 1970s and 1980s and are the subject of Chapter 3. I can give away that there, too, the match between archaeology and Bible is problematic. Now is the turn of David and Solomon, and the questioning of their historicity (Chapter 5).

For the period following these stories, extra-biblical sources are present, texts from Israel itself and from Assyria and Babylonia. Of course, those texts are not necessarily completely reliable. Every inscription has an agenda and gives a specific interpretation of the events described. A good example is the Battle of Kadesh between the Egyptian Pharaoh and the king of Hatti in 1274 BC. Both have written an account of the Battle and each claims victory.

Sitz im Leben

So, if these biblical stories cannot be placed in a historical setting, if they are not historically 'true', why have they ever been written? Who invented or composed them? And when, and for which audience? In other words, what is their *Sitz im Leben*?[1] As usual, scholars agree on some aspects, but not on others. The disciplines of both archaeology and history have recently developed surprising new insights into the background of these narratives.

Traditional Sitz im Leben

Most biblical and archaeological scholars assume that the stories that feature in this chapter have their origins in the Iron Age, even though they may have been written down and edited later. The period of the Exile in Babylon especially would have triggered a need to consolidate the old traditions and to record the history of the people of Judah. Oral traditions and stories, legends and archives were transformed and woven into a grand narrative cycle with a clear historical core.

An example of this trend is the study by the biblical scholar H. Jagersma, *A History of Israel in the Old Testament Period*. This book assumes the historicity of the biblical stories, unless proven otherwise. The *Sitz im Leben* is considered to be the Iron Age, 900–600 BC, for the stories mentioned above, with possible later editions. Jagerma's book is an erudite retelling of the biblical narrative, within a context provided by archaeological finds and texts from Israel and its neighbours.

An archaeologist making the case for the historical reliability of (some of) the biblical stories is William Dever. He has written a book with the ominous title *What Did the Biblical Writers Know and When Did They Know It? What Archaeology Can Tell Us About the Reality of Ancient Israel.* He strongly opposes the minimalist school of thought – see below.

Minimalists

In contrast, some biblical scholars reject any trace of historicity in the biblical narratives. Thomas Thompson, in his book *The Bible in History; How Writers created a Past,* even states that '... the Bible's Israel ... is literary fiction.' We should stop searching for a historical background for these stories, which according to him were mostly written in the Hellenistic period (4th–2nd centuries BC) and focus instead on their theological and literary meaning. Biblical scholars who reject a historical core in the Bible sometimes get the derogatory label of 'minimalists'. The recent past has seen a 'dirty war' between minimalists and their opponents, using archaeology as ammunition.

Brilliant scholars in the 7th century BC

In 2001, Israel Finkelstein and Neil Silberman published a book entitled *The Bible Unearthed: Archaeology's New Vision of Ancient Israel and the Origin of Its Sacred Texts.* The authors claim that the patriarchal narratives were clearly written in the 8th and 7th centuries BC, from the perspective of the kingdom of Judah. They see these stories as a sharp comment on the political condition in the Assyrian and Neo-Babylonian periods. The clear focus on Judah in the book of Genesis is an indication of this background. In the words of the authors:

> It is now evident that the selection of Abraham, with his close connection to Hebron, Judah's earliest royal city, and to Jerusalem ('Salem' in Genesis 14:18), was meant also to emphasize the primacy of Judah even in the earliest eras of Israel's history. It is almost as if an American scripture describing pre-Columbian history placed inordinate attention to Manhattan Island or on the tract of land that would later become Washington D.C. The pointed political meaning of the inclusion of such a detail in a larger narrative at least calls into question its historical credibility.

The authors' conclusion is that the patriarchal traditions should be seen as a 'pious prehistory' of the Israelite people, with Judah as the prime mover. The stories would have been written in Jerusalem in the late 7th century BC by a group of brilliant scribes and scholars. In those days Judah was just a residual state, subdued by first the Assyrians, and after them the Babylonians. To give this desperate people a history, and one that elevated their kingdom on the international stage, was the purpose of this (religious-nationalist) exercise. A historical core is largely missing in these stories, as they rather reflect the ideology of that period. The authors base their dating in the 7th century on numerous details in the stories, which don't fit into earlier or later periods.

One can imagine that this thesis has been heavily criticized. The suggestion that these stories sprouted solely from the imagination of a group of clever scribes at the court in Jerusalem, was a bit too 'innovative'. But it is interesting to see the stories dated solely by archaeological remains, rather than through the 'critical method' (see Chapter 1) for once. But it remains a hypothesis.

An invented history after the Exile

In 2005, the historian Mario Liverani published a book entitled *Israel's History and the History of Israel.* In this fascinating study he presents two versions of the history of ancient Israel. The first is a 'traditional' history based on archaeological remains, inscriptions, Assyrian and Egyptian texts and a critical study of the biblical text. This he calls 'A Normal History'.

The second half of the book addresses the *Sitz im Leben* of the patriarchal stories, the Exodus and the Conquest. Liverani states that these stories were composed after the Exile in Babylon. After his conquest of Babylon, the Persian king Cyrus permitted the exiles to return to their homelands. Not only Judeans were allowed to return (2 Chronicles 36:22–23), but exiles from many different countries, as shown by the Edict of Cyrus, a cuneiform text found in Babylon, and now on display in the British Museum (Fig. 2.7).

The text states:

> From Shuanna I sent back to their places to the city of Ashur and Susa, Akkad, the land of Eshnunna, the city of Zamban, the city of Meturnu, Der, as far as the border of the land of Qutu – the sanctuaries across the river Tigris – whose shrines had earlier become dilapidated, the gods who lived therein, and made permanent sanctuaries for them. I collected together all of their people and returned them to their settlements, and the gods of the land of Sumer and Akkad which Nabonidus – to the fury of the lord of the gods – had brought into Shuanna, at the command of Marduk, the great lord, I returned them unharmed to their cells, in the sanctuaries that make them happy.[2]

However, when the Judean exiles returned in 538 BC, they found not an empty land, as they might have expected, but a fully settled country. There were 'the people of the land', those Judeans that had not been exiled by the Babylonians but had stayed, and still adhered to the ancient Jahwistic religion. Then there were exiles from elsewhere, who had been sent to Judah by the Babylonians. There may also have been Persian and other soldiers who had stayed behind after their campaigns and settled there.

Figure 2.7 The Cyrus cylinder (photo: Mike Peel (www.mikepeel.net) Creative Commons Licence CC BY-SA 4.0).

The stories mentioned above, then, were written to create a possible 'blueprint' for the returnees of how to live together with all these different groups – namely in isolation. The returnees were the chosen people, intermarriages were not permitted, and YHWH was a jealous god. The stories amalgamated ancient folk traditions, historical sources and Babylonian mythological stories into an epic narrative of a people brought by God to the Promised Land (like the exiles by Cyrus), where they had to take on various local groups. Notice the similarity between the Egyptian Sojourn and servitude, the people working on the Pharaoh's great building projects, and the 70 years of exile and servitude in Babylon, working on Nebuchadnezzar's building projects; or the similarity between the Exodus and the return of the exiles from Babylon. Liverani calls this part of his book 'An Invented History', and he even claims that the building of Solomon's temple is an invented story.

You may realise that the same thing is happening again in our time: the Jewish people's return to the Promised Land, the myth of the empty land, the conflicts with the local population, and the old stories being used as justification for a renewed settlement of the land. In the past 30 years the Bible has increasingly dominated this process. That is something that Liverani's devisers of an invented history, or Finkelstein and Silberman's brilliant scribes, would never have foreseen.

Back to the beginning

I am not a biblical scholar myself, but I think it is a bit extreme to dismiss all the stories, from the Patriarchs up to and including the Conquest of the Promised Land (and the building of the Jerusalem temple) as mere fiction. My argument (and that of numerous scholars) is that many of the stories do not fit the historical narrative presented in Deuteronomy. This Bible book focuses on Jerusalem, on the priestly class, and particularly on the temple. No other sanctuaries are allowed and the deity can only be venerated in that particular temple.

However, the older stories in the Bible such as the books of Joshua and Judges are completely unconcerned about other temples, god is venerated on the heights, everywhere in the country local priests have their own sanctuaries, and there is no focus on a central temple, let alone in Jerusalem. That in itself suggests strongly that older threads have been incorporated in what Finkelstein and Silberman call the 'prehistory of Judah'.

And now we are back where we started. What are those older threads, and do they have a historical core or not? But those are not really questions that archaeology can answer; so we will put them back in the biblical scholar's pigeonhole.

Notes

1 In Biblical criticism, *Sitz im Leben* (literally 'setting in life') is a specific term that stands for the alleged context in which a text, or object, has been created, and its function and purpose at that time. It is also used to refer to the social, ethnic and cultural setting of a site during a particular era. When interpreting a text, object, or region, the *Sitz im Leben* has to be taken into consideration in order to allow a proper contextual interpretation.
2 New translation by Irving Finkel, Curator of Cuneiform Collections at the British Museum: http://www.britishmuseum.org/research/collection_online/collection_object_details.aspx?objectId=327188&partId=1.

Chapter 3

In search of ... Saul and the days of the Judges

This chapter describes the period of the Settlement in Canaan and the period of the Judges, starting when Joshua led the Israelites into the Promised Land and conquered Jericho, ending with the crowning of the first king of Israel: Saul (Fig. 3.1). These stories are found in the biblical books of Joshua, Judges and 1 Samuel. Archaeologically speaking this is a fascinating period, because the Early Iron Age, which might be associated with the days of the Judges, saw the birth of numerous villages in the highlands of Israel. A number of those villages have been excavated. On the other hand, king Saul is practically invisible in the archaeological record.

Biblical stories about the settlement and the Judges

The settlement in the Promised Land

After the death of Moses, the Israelites were led into the Promised Land by Joshua and settled in the highlands of Canaan. The book of Joshua recounts the struggle of the people with the Canaanites and the settlement of the 12 tribes. According to the Bible stories, the Israelites travelled through Transjordan and crossed the river Jordan near Jericho. Therefore, Jericho was the first city that had to be conquered and it took a miracle (Joshua 6:13–27). For 6 days the people walked around the city in silence, once daily, while on the seventh day they took seven turns. During the seventh turn the priests blew their ram's horns, the people shouted loudly and the city walls collapsed. Then the Israelites stormed the city and killed everybody – man, woman and child – except for Rahab the prostitute and her family because she had given shelter to the two spies (Joshua 2:1–24). The miraculous fall of Jericho showed beyond doubt that God had given the land to the Israelites.

The conquest of Jericho was the start of a string of bloody wars against the Canaanite inhabitants of the Land, which ended with an Israelite victory, even though Jerusalem was not conquered until the time of King David, and the Philistines in the coastal area remained independent for much longer.

Figure 3.1 Portrait by Rembrandt van Rijn of a bearded man, possibly Saul (Rijksmuseum Amsterdam, public domain).

Judges

Things start to go wrong after Joshua died:

> The Israelites did what is evil in Yahweh's eyes. They forgot Yahweh their God and served Baals and Asherahs. Then Yahweh's anger blazed out against Israel: he handed them over to Cushan-Rishathaim king of Edom, and the Israelites were enslaved to Cushan-Rishathaim for eight years. The Israelites then cried to Yahweh and Yahweh raised for the Israelites a deliverer who rescued them, Othniel son of Kenaz, Caleb's younger brother. The spirit of Yahweh was on him; he became judge in Israel and set out for war. Yahweh delivered Cushan-Rishathaim king of Edom into his hands, and he triumphed over Cushan- Rishathaim. The country then had peace for forty years. (Judges 3:7–11)

After Othniel, God continued to appoint new 'judges' to lead the people. These judges, however, were rarely judges in a judicial sense. They were mainly political leaders and war leaders, taking the front in the many battles that were fought against the Canaanites.

One of the judges was the prophetess Deborah. The position of women seemed to be better in those days than it was later on in the days of the Kings, when women in the towns were confined to their homes. However, the existence of a woman leader does not necessarily mean that ordinary women had much power as well.

The stories in the book of Judges abound in detail about the daily life of the Israelites in their villages, their customs, society, religion and their wars. Because so much more information is given on the daily life in this period compared to later periods, the book of Judges is especially popular in publications with titles such as *Daily Life in Biblical Times*. Often the descriptions given in these publications combine biblical information with excavation results. Whether that is acceptable or not will be discussed below.

Bible and archaeology

Is it acceptable to equate the days of the judges with a historical period, in this case the Early Iron Age or Iron Age I (1200–1000 BC)? This is the same question discussed in the previous chapter with regards to the patriarchal stories; efforts to 'ground' the patriarchs in a historical time frame proved to be not very successful. However, for the days of the judges the situation is different. These biblical stories take place between the Settlement in the Promised Land, a largely mythical narrative, and the days of the Kings, a largely historical period. The days of the Kings coincides with the Late Iron Age or Iron Age II period (1000–587 BC). That would automatically place the days of the Judges in the Early Iron Age.

It turns out that excavations largely confirm the picture of daily life that is painted in the book of Judges (see below). Excavations are of course mute about the appointment of judges by the Lord, their names or noble deeds, or the religious background of these stories, but the descriptions of daily life fit the archaeological record nicely. In their book *The Bible Unearthed,* Israel Finkelstein and Neil Asher Silberman point out that the book of Judges repeats *ad nauseam* the cycle of the people of Israel sinning and then returning to the straight and narrow whenever a new judge is appointed. In the end this hopeless cycle of sin and repentance is broken by the crowning of the first kings, particularly David and Solomon. In the stories the culprits are mostly the ten northern tribes who, as punishment for their sins, eventually disappear, leaving in the Land only the southern tribes of Judah and Benjamin.

We do not know when these stories were written down, whether it was the 7th century BC, as argued by Finkelstein and Silberman, or after the Exile, as assumed by the majority of scholars. But it seems that the period of writing is certainly the time when they received their religious overtones. Nevertheless, the results of archaeological research show that the stories about and perhaps originating in the time when the Israelite tribes settled as farmers in the highlands of Israel, are rooted in the reality of the Early Iron Age. So here we witness a small miracle: (partial) agreement between the Bible and archaeology.

Archaeology

The conquest of Jericho

It was obvious from the start that Jericho would be one of the first targets for archaeological research – those heaps of collapsed walls should be easy to find. In 1868 the English archaeologist Charles Warren was first to visit the oasis of Jericho, where the large mound of Tell es-Sultan was located (Fig. 3.2), and conducted a small excavation. He did not find anything interesting and left soon after. It was not until 1909 that a German team, led by Carl Watzinger and Ernst Sellin, began a major expedition at the site. They found a sequence of substantial walls but had difficulty dating these, so the confirmation of the biblical stories remained in limbo.

To John Garstang, however, excavating at Jericho in six seasons from 1930 onwards, the situation was crystal clear: he found a double city wall, which he dated *c.* 1400 BC, with traces of an earthquake and a conflagration. He decided this must be the remains of the walls destroyed by Joshua.

His discovery created much excitement in Christian circles. Finally, here was confirmation for one of the most miraculous biblical stories. Garstang's dating became the pivot around which numerous efforts to 'historicise' the narrative of the Exodus evolved. If Jericho was destroyed around 1400 BC, the Exodus must have taken place around 1440. Dating the Exodus within either the 13th or the 15th century BC is an ongoing controversy (see Chapter 2).

The picture began to change in 1952 when the famous British archaeologist Kathleen Kenyon began a new series of excavations of the tell. She showed convincingly that the double wall excavated by Garstang was about 1000 years older than he had assumed. Neither in the 15th nor in the 13th century BC had Jericho been densely settled. She found only one isolated building, possibly a farmstead, but no signs of a large walled city.

Figure 3.2 Tell es-Sultan, where ancient Jericho is located. In the foreground is one of Kenyon's deep excavation trenches (Berthold Werner, public domain).

Consternation! How could the biblical story be true if there was no city? Numerous ingenious solutions have been put forward since. One is to push the dating of the Exodus back to the 16th century BC or even earlier when the tell of Jericho was inhabited, so the miracle still stands. Unfortunately, that creates all sorts of problems with the chronology of both Egypt and the Levant. Others have suggested that the remains of the city may have eroded away completely over time which would mean that there was a city in the correct timespan, we just cannot find it anymore. There is a famous saying in archaeological research: 'absence of evidence is not evidence of absence'. This means that if you cannot find something it does not automatically mean that it was never there. But of course, neither does it mean that it *was* there. If we can find no trace of Jericho from the 13th century BC it does not automatically mean that no settlement ever existed in that period, but neither does it prove that there must have been a settlement. Another solution is to state that Tell es-Sultan is not the location of biblical Jericho and that we have to seek the mighty biblical city at another tell.

None of these solutions proved to be very convincing. Maybe the most reasonable explanation is that the biblical account of Jericho's conquest is a much later story. It was included in the Bible to explain how this mighty tell was laying desolate and bare at the junction of two important routes traversing the land of Israel, and to show, of course, that the god of Israel was mightier than the gods of the Canaanites. Biblical verses and archaeological research have their own stories to tell.

Settlements in the Early Iron Age (1200–1000 BC)

Archaeological research has discovered some 120 villages in the hill country of Israel, a small number of which have been excavated. These excavations enable us to piece together a description of contemporary daily life. The villages were fairly small and surrounded by fields. Often the slopes of the hills on which the fields lay were so steep that farmers had to create small terraces. A number of these are still visible in today's landscape. There were no towns in the hill country until much later. Larger settlements were found in the lowlands and along the coast but these were settled by Israel's traditional enemies, the Canaanites and the Philistines.

The village

A village was usually small, around 0.5–1 ha (100 × 100 m maximum) and comprised a number of houses of more or less equal size. There were no public buildings, no central storage facilities, no temples, stables, water systems or fortifications, at least not in Israel. Villages on the other side of the Jordan did have town walls but why they were different is not clear. Khirbet Raddana, for example, one of the excavated

Figure 3.3 Life in an Iron I village. Reconstruction: Semitic Museum, Harvard University and Estate of L. E. Stager; Illustration: C. S. Alexander (Courtesy Semitic Museum).

villages in Israel, consisted of several compounds, each consisting of two or three houses around a central courtyard (Fig. 3.3). One compound would thus house an extended family, consisting of the *pater familias* and his family, the married sons and possibly grandparents and unmarried relatives.

Even though most women gave birth to many children, nuclear families were generally small, usually about four people: a woman, her husband and two children. The combination of high infant mortality and low average age kept the population small. Although women may have borne many children, only a few survived the first few years. It would have been rare to see three generations together in one compound – most people simply did not live long enough to see their grandchildren grow up. On the whole, therefore, a village would house no more than about 150 people. Around the village were the fields and orchards, but also cisterns to collect rainwater, a communal threshing floor, a press for olive oil and another to transform grapes into must and wine.

Houses

The houses in these villages mostly conform to a single type. They are called four-room houses because the ground floor consists of four rooms (Fig. 3.4). The central room was divided into three spaces by two rows of pillars. Often the floor of the central space consisted of compacted earth while the side rooms were cobbled. The fourth room adjoined these three spaces at the back. A stone or wooden staircase led to the upper floor.

The ground floor commonly functioned as a workshop. Here the bread oven and the weaving loom were located, the large grinding stones to grind the corn, and the giant storage jars in which oil and wine were kept. It has been suggested that in winter cattle were also sheltered in the house, in the cobbled side rooms – snug and warm. Stone troughs have been found in some of them which were perhaps used to feed and water the animals.

Cooking was an open-air activity in summer but moved inside in winter. Several houses had two bread ovens: a large one outside in the courtyard, and a small one in the kitchen. The latter also doubled as a stove as winters can get very cold in the hill country. It has been suggested that the central space was not roofed but functioned as an open courtyard. Only the side rooms would have been roofed and that is how the house is often depicted in illustrations. However, more recently, the improbability of this reconstruction has been pointed out. If the central space was open to the elements, rain would also penetrate the side rooms which were, after all, only separated from the central space by a row of pillars. It is more likely that the whole house was roofed, a compelling reason to do the cooking and the baking of bread in the open air in summer.

The upper floor was the living area, where the family resided and slept. It was cooler and lighter than the stuffy ground floor. Biblical texts confirm that people usually slept upstairs – see for example the stories about Elijah and the widow from Zarephath (1 Kings 17:19) and about Elisha (2 Kings 4:11).

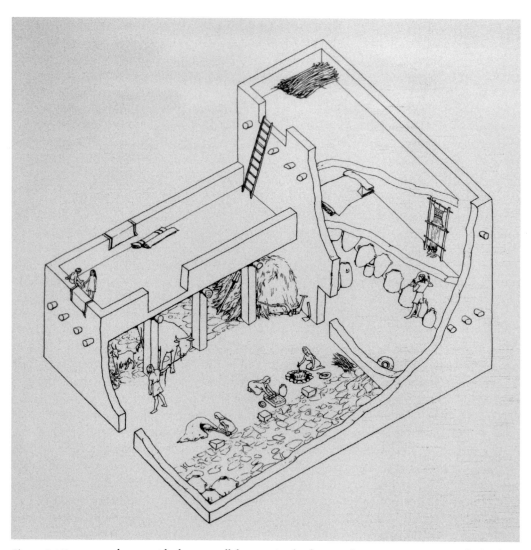

Figure 3.4 Four-room house with three parallel rooms in the front and a transverse room in the back. In this drawing most of the ground floor is left unroofed which is not certain at all. The transverse room may have had a second storey (Chamberi, Creative Commons Licence CC BY-SA 3.0).

Self-sufficiency

The villagers were largely self-sufficient when it came to meeting their daily needs. They had to be, because the cities where they could have bought supplies were all in Canaanite or Philistine territory. Farmers grew mostly wheat and barley which they made into bread and porridge. They cultivated grapes to make wine, and olives for oil. Fruit trees provided them with figs and pomegranates and they kept bees for honey, and goats and sheep for meat and wool. They may also have had an ox to plough the soil and a donkey as beast of burden.

Of course, self-sufficiency was not confined to bringing food to the table. The villagers had to provide their own clothing, furniture, bed linen, table ware and tools. That meant a life full of work, shared by the whole family. Children tended the sheep and goats from a young age and grandmothers spun wool. Women baked the bread but also wove the cloth that dressed the family and made their own crockery and cooking pots. During harvest time the whole family worked in the fields.

Self-sufficiency also extended to other areas of life. There were no teachers, doctors, judges or priests – all these functions were met by the family. Everybody partook in what was needed, from farming to cooking, and from nursing the sick to teaching the young, according to gender, age and ability. The only possible specialisation for which evidence has been found is that of smithing. One of the houses in Khirbet Raddana had a bronze workshop next to it. It consisted of a small kiln, made of a large storage jar, surrounded by broken crucibles with remains of bronze and blowpipes made of clay.

The workshop of Khirbet Raddana was part of a compound of houses with a courtyard that was slightly larger than those of the other compounds. That could mean that it belonged to a slightly wealthier family but not necessarily so. What is certain is that the bronze smith was highly regarded as he had mastered a craft that was not only difficult but vital for the functioning of village life. He crafted tools for the whole village and in return he would receive perhaps a jar of wine, a piece of woven cloth, or home-made cakes. Those tools were mostly made of bronze; iron was still a rare commodity.

Khirbet al-Lehun

Several Early Iron Age villages have also been excavated in Jordan. At Khirbet al-Lehun, in ancient Moab, a Belgian expedition conducted excavations between 1978 and 2000 (Fig. 3.5). The village is dated to the 12th or 11th century BC, the beginning of the Early Iron Age. It extended over 1.7 ha and 23 houses have been wholly or partly excavated. The total number of houses may have been about 60, which makes it a large village compared to those in Israel, such as Khirbet Raddana.

Khirbet al-Lehun also differs from Israelite villages in that it was surrounded by a casemate wall, a double wall with rooms between that could be filled in. The village consisted of four-room houses built against the town wall. The finds were simple: some pottery vessels and storage jars, bread ovens, small grain silos. There were no public buildings, temples or palaces.

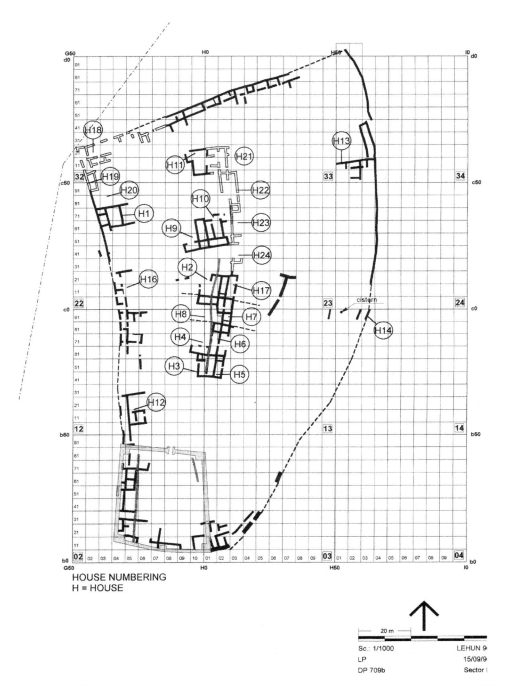

Figure 3.5 Plan of Khirbet al-Lehun with many four-room houses along the perimeter and in the middle of the site. A wall protected the village (courtesy Belgian Committee of Excavations in Jordan).

Figure 3.6 Limestone tablet containing the Gezer calendar (Osama Shukir Muhammed Amin, Creative Commons Licence CC BY-SA 4.0).

The villagers tilled the fields in the wadi next to the village and kept sheep and goats. They were in contact with neighbouring villages and, as members of the same tribe, they would visit each other, exchange marriage partners and join in (religious) festivals. But nothing points to the existence of extensive trade relations with the outer world. Each village seems to have been largely self-sufficient.

Religion

We do not know which gods these villagers, both in Israel and in Jordan, venerated because nothing 'religious' has been found. The farmers in Israelite villages are generally thought to have been YHWH worshippers; this assumption is based on the biblical text and it may well have been the case. The farmers in the Jordanian villages may or may not have been related to the Israelite villagers and they may or may not have had the same religion. All we know is that, several centuries later, the Moabites worshipped Kemosh as their main god.

In this context it may be appropriate to draw attention to the biblical book of Ruth which indicates that, in the days of the Judges, there were close contacts between the Israelites and the Moabites. However, the book of Ruth is difficult to date, that is, to determine when it was written down. It may date from the days of the Kings according to some scholars, or from much later, after the Exile, according to others. It is equally difficult to determine whether the story has a historical core. It is, however, one of the most beautiful stories in the Bible.

Gezer calendar

Central to the life of these farming villages was the yearly agricultural calendar, with its rhythm of ploughing, sowing and harvesting. This cycle is aptly described in an inscription that was found in Gezer, in present-day Israel, in 1908 (Fig. 3.6).

The text is inscribed on a limestone tablet, no larger than 11 × 7 cm, and consists of seven lines. It is not clear whether the language is old Hebrew or Canaanite but that is irrelevant for the content. The text is usually dated to the 10th century BC. It says:

Two months: ingathering. Two months:
Sowing. Two months: late grass.
One month cutting of flax.
One month barley harvest.
One month harvesting and measuring
Two month: pruning (vines).
One month summer-fruit.

This text thus describes the heavy labour of a farming community, over 12 months. The year started with 'ingathering': the harvest of grapes and olives in August or September, which lasted 2 months. After the autumn rains came sowing time. 'Late grass' may refer to a second round of sowing. To make sowing possible the fields had first to be ploughed and proper draining of the terraces organised. The time for harvesting came next: first flax, then barley and finally wheat. Wheat was such an important commodity that the simple word 'harvesting' could be used to refer to the wheat harvest. Next the yield of the harvest was measured. Later, grapes were pruned and at the end of the summer the summer fruit was collected: figs, pomegranates and the like; and then the cycle started again.

Why this stone was thus inscribed is not clear. It is not that the farmers needed to be reminded of the work ahead. Some think it was a writing exercise, for which a common rhyme, maybe sung by children, was used.

Archaeological finds and ethnicity

The four-room building plays an important role in the discussion about the identity (or ethnicity) of the ancient Israelites. What is meant by identity here is whether the Israelites were different from the peoples around them and whether they were aware of these differences or not. In other words, did they have a unique identity and, implicitly, was that identity linked to their religion?

Identity, however, is a difficult subject to describe, even today. There is, for instance, much discussion nowadays among the inhabitants of the Netherlands about whether the Dutch have a unique identity and, if so, what it looks like. Which cultural traits determine Dutch identity? These traits prove hard to identify and to agree on. Determining a unique identity for peoples from an ancient past is even more difficult and, according to some scholars, pointless. Nevertheless, it is a fiercely debated subject.

A trait that distinguished Israelites from other peoples might be, for instance, that they did not eat pork, as this is prohibited in the Bible. Whenever an Iron Age village is excavated the faunal remains are checked for pig bones. If there are any, the village is defined as Canaanite; if there are none, the villagers are supposed to be Israelites honouring the taboo on eating pork.

Unfortunately, things are not that simple. First, this 'rule of thumb' assumes that ancient Israelites knew of this taboo and that they adhered to it as strictly as present-day Jews. Secondly, it assumes that the villages were monocultural, that is, that only followers of the same religion lived in such a village. But who knows, some villages may well have been multicultural.

In the Iron Age pigs were mostly kept in the Shephelah, the lowlands between the hill country in the east and the coastal plain in the west. They are rarely found in the hill country itself. The reason for that may well have been ecological rather than religious or ethnic. Perhaps pigs did not do so well in the hill country? In short, animal bones are not a good marker of identity or ethnicity. This does not mean that some culinary restrictions cannot be identified as 'ethnic or religious markers'. In modern times halal or kosher foods are good examples.

The four-room house used to be seen as an ethnic marker too. Four-room houses were first found in excavations of Early Iron Age villages in the hill country of Israel, and therefore were quickly identified with the Settlement of this region by Israelite tribes; this was a logical conclusion. The next assumption, that these buildings were exclusively Israelite, is more questionable. It assumes that all Israelites built four-room houses and that they were the only ones to do so. Dig up a four-room house and you have found an Israelite family. All you needed to do was look up in the Bible which of the 12 tribes they belonged to.

This idea, obviously, was soon discarded. Villages with four-room houses were increasingly found outside of Israel. The ones in northern Jordan could tentatively be linked to the Israelite tribes that lived east of the Jordan according to the biblical texts but what about those in Israel in areas outside the hill country and those in southern Jordan, Syria and Egypt? It was eventually pointed out that the popularity of the four-room building had perhaps more to do with its functional design, well adapted to farming life, than with any religious or ethnic requirement. Then again, house plans can sometimes be ethnic markers – think of an igloo or tipi or wigwam – but not as a matter of course.

Saul in and outside the Bible

The prophet Samuel was the last judge of Israel. His sons were corrupt and Israel was in perpetual warfare with the Philistines and the peoples of Jordan. Therefore, the people of Israel demanded a king. 'So all the elders of Israel gathered together and came to Samuel at Ramah. They said to him: You are old, and your sons do not follow your ways; now appoint a king to lead us, such as all the other nations have.' (1 Samuel 8:4–5). Samuel resisted but, in the end, gave in and Saul was appointed king of Israel (1 Samuel 10:17–24). His reign would have lasted from c. 1020 to 1000 BC, according to the biblical chronology.

Saul is relatively unknown both within and outside the Bible. There are no inscriptions mentioning his name and no excavated remains can be linked to him. He is 'the forgotten king'. The biblical stories largely focus on his skirmishes with the later 'good king' David and in modern media he is usually represented as the mad or depressive king who needed David's soothing music to find peace.

There have been searches for Saul. According to the Bible he lived in Gibeah, and Gibeah has been excavated. Or rather, Tell el-Ful has been excavated and identified with Gibea (Fig. 3.7). Parts of a square fortress were excavated in 1922, 1933 and 1964. It was dated to the end of the Early Iron Age on the basis of the associated pottery and has

Figure 3.7 Aerial photograph of Tell el-Full, possibly ancient Gibeah, 1931 (Matson Photograph Collection, public domain).

therefore been defined as Saul's fortress. Or was it perhaps the other way round? Was Tell el-Ful identified with Saul's Gibeah, and the associated pottery dated accordingly to the Early Iron Age? No tangible evidence relating the site to Saul has been found so far.

Who were the Israelites?

Earlier in this chapter we looked at the problems arising when we try to reconcile the biblical story of the battle for Jericho with the archaeological record. This is part of a larger problem. In fact, every story in the narrative cycle of Israel's Settlement in the Promised Land is hard to fit into a historical context.

The stories in Joshua and Judges, about wars and destruction, and extermination of the local population seem to have no basis in reality. As with Jericho, many of the 'conquered' cities show no traces of conquest or did not even exist in the period in question. The idea of a wholesale conquest of the land by Hebrews fleeing from Egypt has, therefore, lost a lot of credibility. But if the biblical stories are not 'true', then who were the Israelites and where did they come from?

Peaceful infiltration

As we have seen, archaeological research has revealed many newly established villages in the central hill country of Israel in the 12th and 11th centuries BC. That led scholars to suggest that Israel entered the Promised Land not in an aggressive conquest but as a slow infiltration of groups of people entering from outside and settling in previously unoccupied territory. They came from the east, possibly also all the way from Egypt, crossed the river Jordan and, avoiding the cities in the west, settled in the empty hill country. There they built small villages and lived and worked as farmers.

This means that the Israelites started as a mixture of different groups moving in search of arable land and meeting and settling in the hill country. There they eventually merged and became a single people with a common language and a common religion. This would have been a slow process.

Nomads

Another theory is based on the idea that 'unoccupied' territory in the Near East is rarely empty land. It is often the territory of nomadic tribes who live in tents and use this land for grazing. This way of life is archaeologically almost invisible because it leaves few tangible remains. Nomads build no houses, plant no trees, do not construct olive presses. But they are present. If villages suddenly appear in those 'empty' lands, the most logical explanation is that they were established by these nomads themselves, who began to cultivate the land. This process has occurred regularly in the Levant up until the last century. In times of prosperity nomads settle, cultivate the land and build villages; in times of adversity they leave the land and start wandering again. The same could have happened in the Early Iron Age.

Revolutions

A Marxist-inspired theory states that the new villages were the result of revolutions that had erupted in the Canaanite cities. The slaves and peasants that were suppressed by the local elite revolted and fled to build up a new life in the empty lands. This theory never really took hold because there are no convincing arguments for such an early 'class war'.

Mixed multitude

What it all comes down to is that we do not really know who the Israelites were or where they came from. We do know that they did not exist in the central hill country in the Late Bronze Age (1600–1200 BC) and that they are first mentioned in Assyrian and other inscriptions in the 9th century BC. The centuries between must have seen the birth of this people, as well that of other peoples in the region, such as the Phoenicians, the Ammonites and the Moabites, all of whom had their own (strongly related) languages and their own deities.

Ann Killebrew, in her book *Biblical Peoples and Ethnicity*, calls them a 'mixed multitude', by which she means that the Israelites were formed out of a mixture of different 'elements': nomadic tribes in the process of settling, groups entering from Jordan, fortune hunters, brigands, some refugees from Canaanite towns, and perhaps also a group of slaves who had fled from Egypt and brought their own stories.

Eventually these groups amalgamated into the people of Israel.

Israe'l Stele

An intriguing discovery is the Israel or Merneptah Stele. This inscription was found in Thebes in Egypt in 1896 (fig. 3.8). On this stele Pharaoh Merneptah, who ruled from 1213 till 1203 BC, states that in the fifth year of his reign he dealt with Egypt's enemies.

The last lines of this long text state:

> The princes are prostrate, saying, 'Peace!' Not one is raising his head among the Nine Bows. Now that Tehenu (Libya) has come to ruin, Hatti is pacified;
> The Canaan has been plundered into every sort of woe:
> Ashkelon has been overcome; Gezer has been captured;
> Yano'am is made non-existent. Israel is laid waste and his seed is not;
> Hurru is become a widow because of Egypt.

Figure 3.8 The Israel or Merneptah Stele sound in 1896 (Wellcome Collection Gallery, Creative Commons Licence CC BY 4.0).

The 'nine bows' represent the nine traditional adversaries of Egypt, among them Libya, the Hittites and the Canaanites. Israel is also mentioned: 'his seed is not'. That could mean that its grain reserves were destroyed or it refers to its descendants that were no longer born.

The mystery remains

The appearance of the name Israel in this late 13th century BC text is confusing after having just constructed a neat and tidy history of Israel – the amalgamation of a 'mixed multitude' in the 12th–9th centuries BC. Did there, after all, exist a people of Israel in the 13th century BC, powerful enough to alarm the Egyptian pharaoh? Who were these people, where did they live? And what, if any, is their connection with the later Israelites?

It has been pointed out that the prefix sign that precedes the name Israel on the Israel stele designates a people. This is unlike the prefixes before other names, such as Gezer, Ashkalon and Yanoam, which designate a country or city state. That could mean that Israel was a group of peoples, perhaps a nomadic tribe, or a group of wandering brigands. It is possible that this group eventually became part of the 'mixed multitude' and even gave it its name. Or perhaps the text simply refers to the farming communities that were beginning to settle in the hill country – although this does not explain why Egypt saw them as a threat. The beginning of the biblical Israel is still shrouded in clouds.

serious reservations although the main thread is probably correct: during the reign of Ramesses III Egypt was attacked by a coalition of peoples, from the sea as well as over land. Several battles took place and Egypt prevailed in the end. Somewhat later we encounter several of these peoples in cities along the Levantine coast: the Philistines in the present-day Gaza Strip and further north, and the Tjeker along the Phoenician coast in Dor and Byblos.

Philistines and the Bible

Philistines are mentioned more than 250 times in the Bible. According to these stories they were a people living in the southern coastal plain of Palestine, where they created a league of five of their major cities (the pentapolis), namely Ashkelon, Gaza, Gath, Ashdod and Ekron (see Fig. 6.2). These cities have all been excavated with the exception of Gaza. The Philistines were a powerful people: the biblical narrative abounds with stories about battles against them. Then there is Samson, whose wife was a Philistine woman, and the story of David and his encounter with the Philistine giant Goliath. King Saul was killed in a battle against the Philistines and his body hung from the walls of Beth Shean.

Stories such as that of Samson and the Philistines (Judges 13–16) demonstrate three important characteristics of the Philistines:

1. They are different from Israelites. They live in a different region (the coastal plain), have different gods and different customs; also, they are much more powerful than the Israelites.
2. There is a clear biblical tradition that Philistines came from outside the region, as opposed to the Canaanites, who were the original inhabitants of the land. The Philistines came from over the sea; Caphtor is mentioned several times as their place of origin (Amos 9:7), and this is taken to refer to Crete.
3. A third major difference with the Israelites is that, unlike them, the Philistines were not circumcised. 1 Samuel 18:25 states: 'Saul replied, Say to David, The king wants no other price for the bride than a hundred Philistine foreskins, to take revenge on his enemies.' Saul demanded these foreskins not as an additional act of cruelty against a beaten enemy but as proof that David had really killed Philistines not innocent Israelite peasants. It also enabled Saul to count the number of dead enemies. Egyptians used to cut off the right hand of their dead enemies in order to count them. Piles of hands can be seen on various Egyptian paintings.

Israelites were not the only people who were circumcised. According to the Bible most of their neighbours were too: Moabites, Ammonites, Edomites and Egyptians, as well as 'all the men with shaven temples who live in the desert.' (Jeremiah 9:25). Only Philistines were uncircumcised, a concept perceived as completely alien by the Israelites and as clear proof that they came from elsewhere.

Goliath was the ultimate Philistine. The Bible tells us that 'his height was six cubits and a span. He had a bronze helmet on his head and wore a coat of scale armor of bronze weighing five thousand shekels; on his legs he wore bronze greaves, and a bronze javelin was slung on his back. His spear shaft was like a weaver's rod, and its iron point weighed six hundred shekels' (1 Samuel 17:4–7). This giant, covered from head to toe in heavy armour, was beaten by the shepherd's boy David whose only weapon was a sling and a stone: the classic story of the triumphant underdog.

Excavations at Ekron

Ekron was one of the cities of the Philistine pentapolis. Every city represented a city state with its own hinterland and ruled by its own king. Ashkelon and Gaza were situated directly on the coast while Ashdod, Gath and Ekron lay further inland. Unlike the later Phoenicians, the Philistines were not renowned as traders or seafarers. Only Gaza would eventually, during and after the Iron Age, develop into one of the most important harbours of the Levant. Unfortunately Gaza has barely been excavated.

Ekron (Tel Miqne) has been excavated from 1981 onwards (Fig. 4.4). Much information about the city has been unearthed and fortunately also published. The results can be summarised as follows: in the Late Bronze Age (Strata X–VIII) Ekron was a trade centre. This town was completely destroyed at the end of the 13th century BC. A new, large, walled town was built in the first half of the 12th century BC (Stratum VII), with monochrome 'Mycenaean IIIC' pottery, as described below. The following strata (VI–IV) contained bichrome 'Philistine' pottery. The site consisted of an acropolis

(upper city) and a large lower city, in which a temple was found (see below). The layout of the city, as well as the houses and many of the finds inside the buildings (pottery, loom weights, religious objects) point towards connections with either the Aegean or (more likely) Cyprus. During the 10th century BC this city was destroyed completely.

After the destruction, only the upper city was rebuilt and inhabited (Strata III–II). At the end of the 8th century BC the Assyrians conquered the site, which then became a major production centre for olive oil. During this period the lower city was rebuilt (Stratum I). The Stratum I city was destroyed in 604 BC by king Nebuchadnezzar of Babylon (who also destroyed Jerusalem), never to be rebuilt.

Figure 4.4 Tel Miqne-Ekron, looking north-east, showing Fields of Excavation, July 1996 (photo Ilan Sztulman. Courtesy of Tel Miqne-Ekron Excavation project).

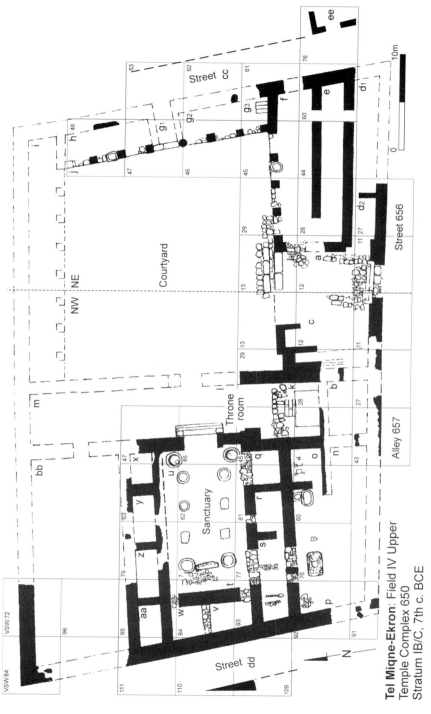

Figure 4.5 Plan of temple 650 at Ekron, Stratum I, 7th century BC (plan prepared by J. Rosenberg. Courtesy of Tel Miqne-Ekron excavations).

Figure 4.6 The Ekron inscription written by king 'Akish (Creative Commons Licence CC BY-SA 3.0).

A dedication inscription for a temple has been found in room U (the sanctuary) of temple 650 of Stratum I (7th century BC) (Figs 4.5 and 4.6), which says:

> This temple was built by 'Akish, son of Padi, son of Yasid, son of Ada, son of Ya'ir, ruler of Ekron, for Ptgyh, his (divine) lady. May she bless him, and guard him, and prolong his days, and bless his land.

The importance of this inscription lies in the fact that it proves that Tel Miqne is indeed Ekron and that it mentions the names of five rulers of the city. It also throws light on the relationship between the king and the deity. The duties of the king include the building of a temple for the deity and the veneration of the deity. The deity, in turn, is obliged to bless and protect the king, lengthen his days and bless the land. *Quid pro quo.*

The same rules are found all over the Middle East, as well as in the Bible (see, for example, Genesis 28:22, which expresses the same sentiment). Jacob builds a sanctuary for God and expects the deity to protect him and provide for him. It is clearly a contract: if God does one thing then Jacob does the other.

The Ekron inscription is written in the Phoenician script, and the language is Phoenician as well. In the Iron Age differences between the written forms of Phoenician, Hebrew, Moabite, Ammonite and Aramaic were rather small.

Pottery (and ethnicity)

Excavations in Philistine cities have yielded significant amounts of pottery that differs significantly from local, earlier Late Bronze Age pottery, as well as from contemporaneous pottery in the surrounding regions. This pottery includes bowls and jars with a painted decoration of lines and circles and sometimes animals, such as dolphins or swans. To put things in perspective: this decorated pottery makes up only about 25% of the pottery found in these cities. Most vessels are not decorated and fit into the common Palestinian repertoire.

Two types of decorated pottery have been found in Ekron (Fig. 4.7). The oldest group, from the lowest Iron Age layers (Stratum VII), is monochrome, using either red or black paint. This pottery group is known in archaeological literature as 'Mycenaean IIIC'. It is found across a large area of the Eastern Mediterranean and particularly in Cyprus. It looks like Mycenaean pottery but has a slightly different

Figure 4.7 Monochrome and bichrome Philistine pottery. The two bowls right and left on the picture are painted with a red decoration on a white-slipped surface. The flask and the handled juglet are decorated with black and red paint on a white slip (Hanay, Creative Commons Licence CC BY-SA 3.0).

decoration. This pottery is ascribed to the groups of immigrants that spread over the Eastern Mediterranean from Greece and its neighbouring areas: the Sea Peoples. They developed their own pottery repertoire inspired by Mycenaean traditions.

The later occupation layers in Ekron (Strata VI–IV) yielded pottery that is designated 'Philistine'. It is close to the monochrome material but is bichrome, using black and red paint on the same vessel, often over a white slip layer. The shapes and decorative motives are also slightly different. It is clear that this pottery was inspired by the earlier monochrome repertoire but developed into a separate, unique style. This repertoire has been found only in the region of the Philistine pentapolis not elsewhere in the Mediterranean.

For a long time scholars thought monochrome pottery found in Ekron had been imported through trade contacts with Cyprus. That would imply that a local population was living in Ekron who valued this pottery and imported it. Only later, when actual Philistines settled in and around Ekron, was 'real' bichrome Philistine pottery produced by them. In other words: monochrome pottery precedes the Philistine occupation while bichrome pottery coincides with the Philistines.

The next step was to identify the pots with the peoples: wherever there was 'Philistine' pottery there must have been Philistines. A single Philistine sherd found on a site would at the least signify contact with Philistines. Conversely, if you did not find any 'Philistine' pottery on a site, that site could not have been home to any Philistines.

However, the relationship between 'pots and peoples' is rather more complex. The first thing to remember is that pottery is made by potters not by the whole population. People can buy pots from 'foreign' potters and, conversely, immigrants can buy their vessels from local potters. Other explanations for the presence of a new type of pottery are also possible, as shown below.

Another complication with the Ekron pottery was that new research revealed that the monochrome pottery had not been imported but was produced locally, using clay from around Ekron itself. So, this was not a case of the imports of fancy pottery by locals. This fancy pottery was made in Ekron itself, probably by 'foreign' potters making their own style of pottery with clay that was available in their new environment. In other words, even before the occurrence of bichrome 'Philistine' pottery there were immigrants in Ekron. That fits in nicely with other finds from these earlier layers: the layout of the fortified city and the style of the temples are all foreign in character. So immigrant Philistines were already present in Ekron in the earlier phase (Stratum VII) and they were the ones who built the Iron Age city.

But perhaps we should take a more general perspective. How do we account for the presence of 'different' pottery in a region? Very often that 'different' pottery is known from elsewhere, or at least looks like it, but sometimes it is a completely new style of pottery. There are a number of different mechanisms that can explain the phenomenon.

Migration

Migration is the most commonly used explanation. Large groups of people move into a different region and bring their own specific type of pottery. In their new country, after they have evicted and/or killed the original population, they continue to make their own pottery and that is how we recognise them. A good example is the introduction of agriculture into Europe by the so-called Linear Pottery Culture. In the 6th millennium BC farmers from the Balkan area migrated westwards as far as the southern Netherlands settling on the fertile loess soils. Their pottery is virtually identical over the whole area in which they settled. But beware: if the pottery that the migrants bring is not significantly different from that of the local population we may never find out about them at all.

Trade

This is a commonly invoked mechanism. Nowadays it is possible, through technological research, to discern whether pottery was made locally or produced elsewhere. The trade in pottery has many aspects. Sometimes pots are traded for their own sake because they are attractive, such as the real Mycenaean pottery in the Levant. At other times they are traded for their content: wine, opium, oil. They may be part of a gift exchange between the elites of different regions or they are wedding gifts exchanged by the local population. In the last two cases the numbers of vessels that are exchanged are probably small.

Diffusion

Sometimes an *idea* is gradually distributed over a wide area, rather than the actual peoples. The introduction of agriculture in the Levant is a good example of this. The practice of cultivation was slowly adopted by hunter-gatherer populations. The same could happen with, for example, the shape of a cooking pot, which potters copied from each other.

Colonisation

A small group of people migrating to a new territory may subjugate the local population. Their customs, pottery, and architecture then become the new norm in the whole region, even though the new rulers form only a small segment of the total population.

Emulation or imitation

Sometimes a group of people imitates the styles and objects of more developed civilizations. For example, the elite of a small country may begin to imitate the beautifully decorated pottery used by the people of a neighbouring powerful state, simply to show they can compete with the big boys. Eventually the rest of the population begins to covet the same pottery, which then puts off the elite from using it. They start to look for other pottery to emulate, and so forth. There are plenty of present-day examples of this mechanism.

Creation

A creative potter may decide to make a different kind of vessel, simply because she wants to. Well-documented examples of this can be found in Mexico where, at the beginning of the 20th century AD, a whole new pottery industry sprang up in this way.

Creolisation

This is the fusion of (elements of) two different cultural traditions into something new. The word was first used to describe the origins of the Creole language, but its meaning has expanded to incorporate other phenomena too.

Acculturation

This describes the process whereby groups of individuals from one culture have long-term contacts with groups of individuals from another culture. Eventually the groups may adopt elements of each other's culture and incorporate these into their own. It will be obvious that these different mechanisms overlap to a certain extent.

So what about the Ekron pottery? Ann Killebrew, in her book *Biblical Peoples and Ethnicity*, discerns three phases in the introduction of the pottery and the arrival of the Philistines.

Phase 1

The arrival of *monochrome* pottery, together with the introduction of other cultural traits as described above (Stratum VII), is the result of migration flows at the beginning of the 12th century BC. A large group of people from Cyprus and surrounding islands settled along the Palestinian coast and built new towns. Their potters continued to produce the same monochrome pottery that they used to make before the move and which was virtually identical in the whole region. It looks like Mycenaean pottery because the migrants who entered the Eastern Mediterranean had their origins in Greece and its surrounding regions. From there they migrated eastwards in the 13th century BC, as part of the Sea Peoples. Although the monochrome pottery looks like Mycenaean pottery it is not identical because Cypriot potters had developed their own unique style.

It is unclear how many migrants entered the country. Perhaps there was a mass immigration, but it is also possible that this was a case of colonisation. Killebrew calls these Philistines 'urban colonists'.

Phase 2

For the development of *bichrome* pottery at the end of the 12th and the beginning of the 11th century BC (Strata VI–IV) we can imagine the following scenario: local potters started to imitate (emulate) the attractive monochrome pottery or perhaps they became apprentices to immigrant potters who were producing the monochrome pottery. Between them, the local and immigrant potters developed a new pottery style, the bichrome 'Philistine' pottery, which is therefore the wrong epithet. The new style displays elements of the older monochrome pottery (the decoration, sometimes the shape), with new Cypriot influences (the white slip layer) and with local elements as well (the bichrome decoration and sometimes the shape). It is a clear case of creolisation. We have to keep in mind that whilst this pottery is found in the cities ruled by the Philistines, it may have been made by potters from all backgrounds.

Phase 3

During the 10th–7th centuries BC a process of acculturation took place. The Philistines increasingly adopted elements from the local culture. By the end of the Iron Age they have largely lost their distinctive identity, as regards their material culture. The pottery produced at their sites now looks the same as in the rest of the country.

So we see here several mechanisms at work, consecutively colonisation, emulation, creolisation and acculturation.

One would expect Philistine pottery, attractive as it was, to be in great demand in other regions. However, elsewhere in ancient Israel and in the areas around it, hardly a sherd of Philistine pottery has been found, even in sites that (according to the Bible) were Philistine strongholds, such as Beth-Shean. Only a few burial sites contained the occasional bichrome vessel. The dearth of Philistine pottery contrasts with Cypriot and Phoenician pottery, which was popular in the whole region. Philistine pottery was neither imported nor imitated elsewhere. Interestingly, this 'problem' has largely been ignored in archaeological literature.

Has Goliath been found?

In 2005, during the excavations at Tel es-Safi in Israel, identified with the Philistine city of Gath, an ostracon was found – that is a pot sherd with an inscription written on it in ink, often a copy of a letter or a writing exercise (Fig. 4.8). This particular inscription caused much excitement. Bar

Figure 4.8 'Goliath' ostracon found in Gath (photo: Vladimir Naikhin. Courtesy Tell es-Safi/Gath Archaeological Project).

Ilan University issued a press release saying: 'The discovery is of particular importance since the Bible attributes Gath as the home of Goliath. [...] The archaeological find may also be seen as the first clear extra-Biblical evidence of the well-known Biblical story of the battle between David and Goliath.'

By now you know the rules of the parlour game: an archaeological find supporting a detail within a Bible story – in this case the name of Goliath – thereby confirms the historical reliability of the whole story (the fight between David and Goliath), and in effect of the whole biblical narrative.

The scientific community quickly came to its senses. In 2006, dig director Aron Maeir wrote on his blog: 'The inscription demonstrates that ca. the 10th/9th century BCE, names very similar to Goliath were in use at Philistine Gath. This does provide some cultural background for the David/Goliath story.'

So what is this all about? As we have seen, we do not know what language the Philistines spoke or what script they used. Philistine inscriptions from the Early Iron Age (12th–10th centuries BC) have never been found. The 'Goliath-inscription' dates from the 10th or 9th century BC, which makes it special and important. It is not written in the unknown Philistine script but in an early form of the script which was used by Phoenicians and Israelites.

The inscription itself consists of a few letters: A L W T W L T. This could represent two names: 'Alwt' and 'Wlt'. Scholars had already concluded that the name Goliath, as found in the Bible, does not have a Semitic root. It could be the Semitic spelling of an Indo-European name, which would then have been something like 'Aylattes'. The two names on the sherd show the same structure and could both be variants of this name Aylattes – in other words, of Goliath. But neither name on the sherd is really Aylattes.

This is all very interesting and it confirms that the name Goliath (or a variation thereof) was a name found among the Philistines. However, an endorsement of the fight between the shepherd boy David and the Philistine giant demands a little more evidence. Of course, absence of evidence is not evidence of absence: we cannot say that these things did *not* happen, we just don't have the evidence to prove they did.

Religion of the Philistines

Little is known of the religion of the Philistines. The Bible mentions *Dagon,* the god whose temple in Ashdod received the Ark of the Covenant after the Philistines had captured it. The story, in 1 Samuel 5, is too good to be missed (notice in particular the *hemorrhoids* with which God smote the Philistines of Ashdod). Dagon is a Canaanite deity already encountered in the Ugarit texts from the Late Bronze Age. It is curious that the Philistines from 'across the sea' would have elevated a Canaanite god to be their supreme deity.

Another god mentioned in the Bible is *Baal-Zebub,* the god of Ekron (2 Kings 1:2). Baal-Zebub may be translated as Lord of the Flies and is often seen as a biblical derogatory wordplay on *Baal-Zebul,* Lord of the House (the temple). Also mentioned

Figure 4.9 The Ashdoda: a small figurine of a woman sitting on a chair or throne. As the name reveals, she was excavated at Ashdod (Creative Commons Licence CC BY-SA 3.0).

in the Bible is *Astarte,* whose temple stood in Beth Shean (1 Samuel 31:10). Both Baal-Zebub (or Baal-Zebul) and Astarte are the names of Canaanite and later Phoenician deities.

The archaeological record, gainsaying the biblical stories, suggest that the main deity of the Philistines was female, a goddess. The inscription mentioned below speaks of 'Ptgyh the divine lady'. Since no goddess of that name is known from elsewhere, this line has been the subject of much hypothesising of exactly what the inscription says and what the letters mean. Most scholars agree that it refers to a goddess, even though her name is speculative and her origins are unknown.

Large numbers of figurines have been found in every Philistine city: small statuettes of women made of clay. In itself this is not spectacular; female figurines have also been found in the later Iron

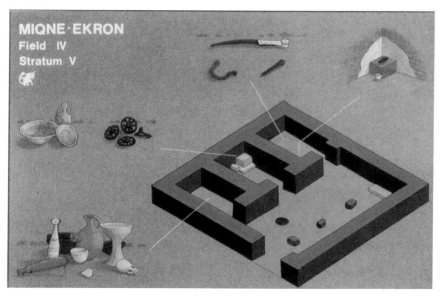

Figure 4.10 Temple excavated in strata VI–IV at Ekron (Courtesy Tel Miqne-Ekron Excavations).

Age in the cities of Israel and Judah (see Chapter 10). But in Ashdod, a beautifully decorated statuette has been found depicting a woman sitting on a chair (or throne?). The two elements, woman and chair, have merged into one. She is named after the place where she was found: 'Ashdoda' (Fig. 4.9). Like the Philistine pottery she is covered with white slip and painted in two colours (red and black).

In Ekron another temple was excavated in Strata VI–IV, which formed part of a larger complex of buildings (Fig. 4.10). The temple has a hearth on the courtyard (a common feature in Greece and on Cyprus), and an iron knife was found in it which will be discussed below.

This temple had two phases. In the latest phase, dating to the 11th century BC, the building consisted of a forecourt with two pillars. This forecourt led into a courtyard with three pillars and a circular hearth. Three rooms surrounded this courtyard. The middle one contained a platform which probably carried the statue of the deity. The other rooms were store-rooms for the cult paraphernalia and the gifts and donations to the temple. In the earlier phase, of the 12th century BC, the temple was smaller, with a very large hearth in the forecourt. We do not know which god was venerated in this temple. Temples like these have also been found in other Philistine cities, such as Tell Qasile and Tel es-Safi (Gath).

Philistines and iron

It is often claimed that the Philistines had a monopoly on iron; arguments for this are taken from the Bible. The Philistines would have copied the art of iron smelting from the Hittites when they invaded their country and taken the 'secret' with them to the Levant. They were therefore capable of making iron weapons which gave them a great advantage over their enemies who had to make do with bronze weapons. Take, for example, Goliath, who is described in the bible as having an iron spearhead.

There is, of course, a reason for calling the Iron Age just that. The production of iron starts around 1200 BC when it gradually began to replace bronze for weapons and tools. But it took several centuries before this replacement really took hold.

However, the idea that the Philistines had mastered and exploited the secrets of iron production is not as straightforward as it seems. First of all, contrary to what many people think, the biblical stories do not say that. In 1 Samuel 13:19, for example, it says: 'Not a blacksmith could be found in the whole land of Israel, because the Philistines had said, Otherwise the Hebrews will make swords or spears.' Iron is not mentioned at all here, this text is about weapons. And in those days, weapons were still made of bronze.

Secondly, excavations have shown that there actually *were* smiths in Israel (see Chapter 3). The idea that the Philistines in their cities could prohibit smiths and smithing in the Israelite villages is in itself ludicrous. However would they enforce that? A bigger problem is that iron in its early days was not better than bronze. We

Figure 4.11 Iron knife with ivory handle, found in the temple of Stratum V at Ekron (photo: Ilan Sztulman. Courtesy Tel Miqne-Ekron Excavations).

are talking here about cast iron which is rather soft. Only later, when smiths started to add charcoal or dung to the iron bloom and so created an early form of steel, did the quality improve. This steel was a superior product compared to bronze, but cast iron was not.

A beautiful cast iron knife was found in the temple in Ekron (Fig. 4.11). Its length is *c.* 50 cm, and it has an ivory haft riveted with bronze (!) nails. However, the knife itself would have been too fragile to have ever been used as a weapon. It more likely had a ceremonial function.

This begs the question, what triggered the transition from bronze to iron? The most likely answer is that towards the end of the Late Bronze Age the supply lines were cut by the Sea Peoples and their attacks. Bronze is an amalgamation of copper and tin, two elements that are never found together in the same location. Sea trade was pretty much a precondition for bronze production. After the trade was interrupted there was still enough bronze around to last for quite a while. A broken bronze sword could be melted down and made into a new sword. But eventually people had to look for new metals. Iron was known from meteorites and as a by-product of bronze production. Iron ore is very common, so iron was worth developing further. Still, throughout the Iron Age bronze remained a common product (as were flint tools).

So there was a solid reason for the biblical warrior Goliath to wear a helmet, armour and weapons made of bronze: they were much safer.

Who were the Philistines?

All in all the origins of the Philistines remain shrouded in mystery. Both the biblical texts and Egyptian and other inscriptions are adamant that they are not indigenous in the Levant but prove uncertain of their region of origin. Most likely they were on the move as part of process of mass migration occurring during the 13th and 12th centuries BC in the Eastern Mediterranean. As no inscriptions have been found from this period written by the Philistines themselves, their language is unknown. The only excavated inscription dates to the 7th century BC and is written in Phoenician.

Archaeology has encountered the Philistines and other Sea peoples along the coast of the Levant, where they settled during the 12th century BC. The lay-out of their towns, their temples and their pottery show connections with the Aegean and Cyprus. Slowly they integrated into the local culture.

Chapter 5

In search of ... David and Solomon

This chapter enters into the discussion about kings David and Solomon. In the Bible they represent the Golden Age of Ancient Israel, when the kingdom was united, their kings were strong and wise, and prosperity abounded (Fig. 5.1).

Unfortunately, extra-biblical sources are almost silent on these two kings. The more the Bible has to say about a king, the less we hear of him outside the Bible, it seems. The excavation of the so-called 'palace of king David' in Jerusalem caused an uproar but did not solve the paradox.

David and Solomon in the Bible

The narrative cycles about David and Solomon provide us with some of the most enchanting stories the Bible has to offer. The stories are detailed, exciting, intimate and personal: David the shepherd boy who ends up as king of Israel; his complicated relationship with king Saul; his love for Saul's son Jonathan; the fight against Goliath; his love life; David the lyre player, the poet of the Psalms. When he dances in front of the Ark of the Covenant on its return to the city, he is so excited that his private parts are exposed, to the contempt of his wife Michal; David, who fasts and sleeps on the floor for nights on end, when his little son falls ill. All these stories are found in 1 and 2 Samuel. David is a warrior, a fighter. He unites the tribes into one kingdom, conquers Jerusalem, taking it from the Jebusites and he leads a turbulent private life, to put it mildly.

Solomon, on the other hand, is the ideal king: wise, powerful and rich. Solomon is not a warrior, he is a builder. The Bible mentions his building projects in Jerusalem: the temple, his palace, the palace for Pharaoh's daughter. He builds Etzion-Geber on the gulf of Aqaba/Eilat, and the cities of Gezer, Hazor and Megiddo. He consolidates the empire his father conquered, tightens diplomatic relations with neighbouring countries such as Egypt and the Phoenician cities through marriages with foreign princesses and enriches the country with numerous trade expeditions. 1 Kings 2–11 reads like a fairytale.

Figure 5.1 King David monument in Jerusalem (Fallaner, Creative Commons Licence CC BY-SA 4.0).

In the Bible the Golden Age of Israel ends with Solomon's son Rehoboam. During his reign the 'United Kingdom' falls apart into two separate kingdoms: the northern kingdom of Israel and the southern of Judah. The kings of 'the house of David' continue to rule in Judah, whilst in Israel, usurpers take over. We will meet them below in chapter 6, which is about queen Jezebel and the 'house of Omri'.

Traditionally it is assumed that the biblical stories about David and Solomon were based on court chronicles, taken to Babylon by the exiles and edited during the Exile. After all, the argument goes, the stories are so detailed that they *must* be based on old records. For other scholars, however, the same detail proves that the stories were invented, as court chronicles would never record small matters of this kind.

A comparison with the stories on the later kings of Judah may clarify this point. Take, for example, the deeds of Asa, the great-grandson of king Solomon, as narrated in 1 Kings 15:9–24 and 2 Chronicles 13–16. These stories record only battles, building projects, victories and defeats, and religious matters; the things with which a king should concern himself. These texts are comparable to the Mesha Stele (a large upright stone), an inscription dated to the 9th century BC, which enumerates the deeds of king Mesha of Moab in his own words. There is not a word in the Mesha Stele on the king's emotions, his love life, his joys or his sorrows, let alone his private parts. This inscription is discussed in chapter 7.

There are no direct clues in the Bible as to when David and Solomon lived. Usually their place in time is calculated as follows: the destruction of Jerusalem by the Babylonians almost certainly took place in 587 BC. From here it is possible to count back by adding up the reigns of the kings of Judah. Ultimately this will lead you to the reign of king David, which would then fall between 1000 and 950 BC. His son Solomon reigned *c.* 950–920 BC. In archaeological terms this is the beginning of the Late Iron Age.

But beware: the fact that it is possible to calculate these dates does not mean that 'therefore' David and Solomon are historical figures who actually lived in those years. It is a calculation based on biblical texts, which has value only within the context of those texts, unless there is extra-biblical supporting evidence.

David and Solomon outside of the Bible

The wealth of information in the Bible on David and Solomon is in stark contrast to an almost complete silence with regard to these kings outside the Bible. Neither the Assyrian nor the Egyptian sources mention David's campaigns or Solomon's vast empire, which stretched from Egypt all the way to the Euphrates. That, in itself, does not necessarily mean much, since there are relatively few Egyptian and Assyrian sources from the 10th century BC.

The only exception is a stele found in Tel Dan in the far north of Israel (Figs 5.2 and 5.3). Several fragments of the broken stone slab were excavated in 1994, which

Figure 5.2 Photograph of the Tel Dan inscription mentioning the 'House of David' (Yoav Dothan GFDL http://www.gnu.org/copyleft/fdl.html).

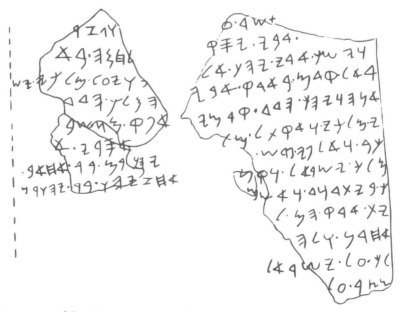

Figure 5.3 Drawing of the Tel Dan inscription (Schreiber, Creative Commons Licence CC BY-SA 3.0).

had been reused as building stones in a large wall. In the stone an inscription had been cut. The wall dates from the 8th century BC, while the stele itself is dated to the 9th century BC, a date based on the shape of the letters. The language used is Aramaic.

A large part of the text is missing. What is left of the text can be translated as follows:

> [...] and cut [...]
> [...] my father went up against him in war at [...]
> And my father lay down and he went to his fathers. Now the king of
> Israel had gone formerly into the land of my father. But, then, as for me, Hadad made
>   me king.
> And Hadad went before me, and I departed from the seven [...
> ...] my kingdom and I killed [seve]nty kings who harnessed [thousands of
> char]iots and thousands of horsemen. [I killed Jeho]ram son of [Ahab]
> King of Israel, and I killed [Ahaz]iahu son of [Jehoram]
> **king of the house of David**. And I made [their towns into ruins and turned]
> their land into [...]
> other [...]
> over Israel [...]
> siege upon [...]

On the face of it, the text does not make much sense. It was probably a victory stele commissioned by an Aramaic king after he had conquered the city of Dan. Hadad was the god who made it all possible. Two kings were killed in battle, which are mentioned by name: Jehoram, son of Ahab, king of the northern kingdom of Israel, and Achazjahu, king of the house of David, which was the southern kingdom of Judah. You will notice that large parts of each of the names are missing, but the remaining '....ram' and '...jahu' are the defining clues. There is only one combination of kings of Israel and Judah reigning at the same time, and whose names (in Hebrew) ended in '...ram' and '...jahu', respectively. That makes it possible to complete the names, and at the same time to place the events mentioned in the text at the end of the 9th century BC.

The text's main significance derives from the letters BYTDWD: Beth David, House of David (emboldened text above). This is not a reference to a dynasty, as in the House of Hanover, but rather a geographic denotation. In Assyrian texts the northern kingdom of Israel is often designated as *Beth Omri*, the House of Omri. In the text the House of David is placed in opposition to Israel, mentioned in the previous lines, and therefore it most likely means the southern kingdom of Judah. This is the earliest extra-biblical mention of the name of David.

It will not surprise you that this discovery generated a much heated debate, ranging from 'undisputed evidence for the historical David' at one end of the spectrum, to 'has to be a forgery' at the other end. Some of the main issues that shape this discussion are:

- The words 'House of David' as a designation for the kingdom of Judah may indicate that David was generally held to be the founder of the kingdom, comparable to Omri of Israel (see Chapter 6).
- On the other hand, the designation 'House of David' for the kingdom of Judah is not found in any Assyrian inscription.
- All words in the inscription are separated by a dot, which functions as a word divider. But there is no divider between the words 'House' and 'David'. This has given rise to other translations of the word, such as 'Temple of (the deity) Dod' or a place name.
- The earliest possible date for the inscription is the end of the 9th century BC, almost a century and a half after David lived, according to the biblical chronology.

The text does not necessarily prove that David existed, as the period between the time that this biblical king may have lived and the writing of the text is quite long. It does, however, mention, David in connection with the kingdom of Judah. I think that the only conclusion we can draw from the inscription with any certainty, is that at the end of the 9th century BC David was seen as the (perhaps mythical) founder of the southern kingdom of Judah.

Archaeological excavations

The archaeology of the time of David and Solomon, the days of the United Monarchy in the 10th century BC according to the Bible, is (again) a hot topic in literature and on the internet. In short, the situation is as follows:

During the 1950s and '60s neither the historicity of both kings nor the extent of their empire was doubted by many. After all, the picture that was painted in the biblical stories was nicely confirmed by archaeology. Or so it seemed. The procedure went as follows: If you excavated a city that had a connection in the Bible with one of the two kings, that city would then automatically be dated to the 10th century BC by the excavators. For example, in Megiddo (Fig. 5.4), Hazor and Gezer city gates were excavated which were all of the same type, with six chambers. I Kings 9:15 tells us that Solomon was responsible for the building of these three cities, so it 'follows' that these gates and the stratum they belonged to, were built by king Solomon and thus dated to the second half of the 10th century BC. Pottery from these layers was then dated to that time as well. All of this was seen as evidence that David and Solomon ruled over a vast empire, just as the Bible tells us. You date a city based on the biblical stories and then you claim that the biblical stories are true. What circular reasoning ...?

But then radiocarbon dating changed everything. Many of the buildings that had been ascribed to king Solomon on the basis of the biblical text, turned out to be a century younger. As a result, large cities and palaces that had been ascribed to the

Figure 5.4 Aerial photograph of Tel Megiddo (Avram Graicer Creative Commons Licence CC BY-SA 3.0).

10th century BC were suddenly transported to the 9th century instead. So what did that leave for the 10th century? Very little indeed. Some archaeologists now claim that in the 10th century BC Judah was a rural area with no more than a few thousand inhabitants, and that Jerusalem was little more than a village.

However, advances in research usually lead to advanced understanding and insight. Recent progress in radiocarbon dating methods has refined the older dates and some of these palaces and occupation layers have now been redated back to the 10th century BC – albeit not unchallenged. Since the discovery of those first three six-chambered gates at Megiddo, Hazor and Gezer, several more have been excavated, both in Israel and elsewhere. These gates date to different periods,and cannot possibly be linked to Solomon – for example the town gate of Mudayna Thamad in Jordan (Chapter 7).

An additional problem is posited by the pottery from excavated layers. You may think that pottery is used to date these layers and you are right to do so. However, pottery does not have a fixed date written on it, so first of all the pottery itself needs to be dated. However, it is dated on the basis of the occupation layers in which it is found – more circular reasoning. The pottery from the cities of Megiddo and Hazor was considered to be typical for the 10th century BC because the Bible says that those cities were built by king Solomon. That was how this pottery got its date, after which it could be used to date other cities.

However, if the dating of Megiddo and Hazor shifts downwards, based on radiocarbon dating, the dating of the pottery shifts with it and the whole construct begins to slide. Some archaeologists stick to the traditional dates (the 'high chronology') which implies that a certain type of attractive red-burnished pottery belongs to the 10th century BC; others have adopted a 'low chronology', dating that same pottery to the 9th century BC. The occupation layers ascribed to Solomon in the traditional 'high' chronology are dated to the time of king Ahab in the 'low' chronology. As a result there are no occupation layers left for king Solomon's building projects.

What you need to keep in mind is that these chronological squabbles have little impact on the history of the region in so far as it is based on the archaeological record. Whether a particular layer is dated to the second half of the 10th or the beginning of the 9th century BC is not terribly important. More interesting for archaeologists are questions about the transition from a rural to an urban society, the functions of the cities and their layout, and the nature of the trade relations between Judah, Israel and the surrounding regions. The discussion about a 'high' or 'low' chronology only becomes relevant in relation to the biblical kings David and Solomon.

In order to make the relationship between archaeology and the biblical narrative a bit more tangible, I will focus on three specific problems: Solomon's stables, which were found in Megiddo, the Palace of David, claimed to have been found in Jerusalem, and the excavations at Khirbet Qeiyafa, said to have proven that the Bible was right.

Solomon's stables

A particular group of buildings found in the 1920s, the so-called 'Stables of Megiddo', led to a heated polemic. The buildings consist of three parallel aisles with pillars between (Fig. 5.5). Between the pillars stood stone troughs (Fig. 5.6). The excavator interpreted these buildings as stables for horses and related them to biblical texts that refer to king Solomon's horsemen: 'Solomon had four thousand stalls for chariot horses, and twelve thousand horses.' (1 Kings 4:26).

However, modern ideas about these buildings are more nuanced. For one thing, the dating of the stables does not fit the biblical text (according to the 'low' chronology the stables would be later). Apart from that, the ground plan of the building does not seem very suited for stabling horses. The horses would have to jump over their troughs to get into their box or they would have to be walked all the way around behind the other horses. So that should have been the end of the theory of the stables.

However, some recently published articles have revived the idea. Comparing these stables with examples in other parts of the world has shown that horses may have been kept in these structures. Of course this does not prove that they were, but it is possible. This still leaves the dating, and thus the connection with the biblical texts, in limbo. If the buildings are not from the 10th century BC they cannot be connected to king Solomon.

Besides that, after the discoveries at Megiddo, comparable buildings have been found in other towns, either with or without troughs between the pillars. Some of these buildings were clearly used for storage, such as those in Beersheba; other may

Figure 5.5 Reconstruction of Megiddo in the Iron Age. The stables are front right (photo: Immanuel Giel (CC BY-SA 4.0)).

Figure 5.6 Artistic reconstruction of trough with horse at the tel (Immanuel Giel, Creative Commons Licence CC BY-SA 4.0).

Figure 5.7 Pillared building at Mudayna Thamad with the lintels still in place. Remains of limestone troughs are visible between the pillars (photo: Noor Mulder).

have been indoor markets, or army barracks. In Khirbet al-Mudayna in Jordan pillared buildings with troughs have been excavated which clearly had an industrial function, possibly in textile production; the troughs are too high for horses to be able to drink from them (Fig. 5.7).

The 'stables' at Megiddo may indeed have been stables, or they may have had another function. They may be dating from the 10th century BC or from the 9th. Either way, their relation with the biblical texts is tenuous at best.

King David's palace

In 2005 archaeologist Eilat Mazar announced that she had excavated king David's Palace in Jerusalem. The palace is mentioned several times in the Bible, for instance in 2 Samuel 5:11: 'King Hiram of Tyre sent envoys to David, with cedar logs, carpenters and stonemasons; and they built a palace for David.' Mazar used various biblical texts to work out where the palace had to have been located in the city. She then started a dig and found several substantially built walls which, according to her, could only belong to a palace. She also found pottery which she dated in the 10th century BC.

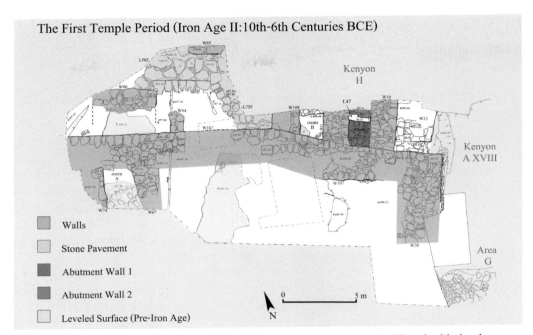

The First Temple Period (Iron Age II:10th-6th Centuries BCE)

Walls

Stone Pavement

Abutment Wall 1

Abutment Wall 2

Leveled Surface (Pre-Iron Age)

Figure 5.8 Drawing of the 'Palace of king David' with the walls of the building highlighted in grey (copyright Eilat Mazar).

The news that the palace of king David had been excavated caused much upheaval. It was announced in newspapers all over the world, from the *Jerusalem Post* to the *New York Times*. The leading article in the *National Geographic* of 2010 was dedicated to king David and his palace. A fierce debate also raged on various websites, from orthodox Christian organisations to sceptical 'free thinking' websites. They all announced the spectacular find as proof that 'the Bible is History', or just the opposite!

Was Mazar right when she claimed that she had found the palace of king David? The plan of the walls she excavated seems convincing at first sight (Fig. 5.8): an imposing building, on top of a hill, on a well protected spot. But in order to prove that she really excavated king David's palace, we would need more evidence, such as:

1. There has to be a real large building. A few isolated walls are not enough.
2. It needs to be proven that this building is actually a palace. How does one prove that something is a palace? Ideally, you'd find an inscription or a throne room. A royal archive would be helpful too. But nothing of the kind has been found.
3. Once the palace has been identified it needs to be dated to the correct period. The usual way is through pottery. As we have seen above, however, this is problematic, because archaeologists cannot agree on which exactly pottery should be dated to the 10th century BC. For radiocarbon dating you need carbonised organic remains, which were not found.

4. Finally, if a palace dating to the correct period has actually been excavated, it still need to proven that it was king David who lived there. Since we're not even sure that king David actually existed, it would need at least an inscription to tell us that.

Using the criteria above, the question remains of whether Eilat Mazar has furnished those proofs. Let us take them one by one.

1. From what I can see, Mazar excavated some very large walls but not a real building. A closer look at the published plan reveals this (Figs 5.8 and 5.9). At first sight there seems to be a giant building, with walls about a metre thick (highlighted in grey). However, ignoring the highlighting and looking carefully at the actual stones that have been found, the picture changes. Only a few fragments of really substantial wall were excavated, whilst other fragments are much thinner, or missing altogether. Also, the orientation of the walls varies, and some do not even connect with one another.

   The published drawings and photos show three different wall complexes: to the north, the west and the east side of the 'building'. The western complex is part of an area excavated in the 1920s by the British archaeologist R. A. S. Macalister, who found a building from the Hellenistic period there. According to researchers from Tel Aviv University, who compared Mazar's discovery with Macalister's original plans, she has actually re-excavated those Hellenistic walls.

   The northern wall complex is located in an area that was excavated by Kathleen Kenyon in the 1960s, and published by myself. I therefore compared the walls and floors excavated by Mazar with those of Kenyon's original files, after which I had to conclude that Mazar (again) had re-excavated older walls. These walls date mostly to the Middle Bronze Age and are therefore some 800 years older than Mazar claimed.

   On the east side, again, Mazar re-excavated walls that were originally excavated by Kenyon. These walls can indeed be dated to the Iron Age but they form only a small part of the so-called palace. In other words, critical analysis indicates that the walls that Mazar excavated as being part of one and the same building, actually belong to different buildings and date to different periods.

2. Did Mazar demonstrate that there really was a palace? The evidence reviewed above shows that she did not convincingly demonstrate that her walls belong to a single building so that theory would seem unsustainable.

3. Mazar stated that she had difficulty dating the walls, because she did not find floors belonging to them. The reason for this is that previous excavations had often removed the layers between the walls, only leaving the walls themselves so the absence of floors should not really have come as a surprise. In some places where Mazar dug deeper than her predecessors she did find floors, with pottery dated to the Middle Bronze Age (around 1800 BC) and the Early Iron Age (1200–1000 BC). However, those floors are situated below the walls of the 'palace' and are therefore older. Mazar dates the pottery she recovered to the 10th century BC but the assemblage

Figure 5.9 Substantial walls excavated in the so-called Palace of David. They belong to different periods, however (photo: Margreet Steiner).

includes sherds belonging to the Early Iron Age which would pre-date king David. Some sherds do indeed belong in the 10th century, but they were found in a fill layer between two walls not on a surface so probably do not date construction or original use.

4. Has the palace of king David been excavated? In my opinion it probably has not.

Khirbet Qeiyafa

Repeatedly new discoveries are presented as proof that king David did exist and that the biblical stories about him are historically accurate. One of the more recent, and certainly the most sensational, is the excavation of a site called Khirbet Qeiyafa. The excavators present their excavation results as spectacular findings throwing new light on the history of ancient Israel.

Qeiyafa is a small site of 2.5 ha overlooking the Elah Valley west of Jerusalem (Fig. 5.10). It was occupied in the late 11th–early 10th centuries BC and the excavators identified it with biblical Shaara'im, mentioned in 1 Samuel 17:52 in connection with the story of David and Goliath: 'Then the men of Israel and Judah surged forward

Figure 5.10 Aerial photograph of fortress Khirbet Qeiyafa (Creative Commons Licence CC BY-SA 4.0).

with a shout and pursued the Philistines to the entrance of Gath and to the gates of Ekron. Their dead were strewn along the road to Shaara'im, as far as Gath and Ekron.' This identification rests mainly on the name of the biblical town, meaning 'with two gates'. Qeiyafa has town walls with two gates, according to the excavators, and is located not far from the Philistine towns of Ekron and Gath, so it may well be biblical Shaara'im.

Qeiyafa would have been an outpost of Jerusalem, and 'thus' proof that Jerusalem was a considerable city in the 10th century BC. This could then also be seen as proof that king David existed and ruled over a large area. An ostracon (inscription with ink on a pot sherd) was found that would have been written in Old Hebrew and that mentions the words 'king' and 'slave': another piece of evidence that the inhabitants were Judeans living in king David's large empire.

However, archaeologists from Tel Aviv University published a scathing article stating that the second gate is not a gate at all, that the large city wall does not stem from the Iron Age but is Hellenistic in date, and the identification with Shaara'im is therefore incorrect. They suggested further that the inhabitants of the site were not Judeans, as most pottery and other finds have more connections with the northern part of Israel and with Transjordan than with sites in Judah, and that there is no proof that it was an outpost of Jerusalem. Other have raised doubt on the language of the ostracon and claim it is written not in Hebrew but in Phoenician, Canaanite or Moabite.

In 2013 another spectacular find at the site was announced by the Israel Antiquities Authority: a palace was uncovered belonging to and used occasionally by king David. The king really slept there sometimes! However, no clear proof was presented to support these assertions.

However interesting the excavations at Khirbet Qeiyafa are, the claims of the excavators could not be substantiated and rest solely on a creative interpretation of the findings. They did not excavate any tangible evidence of king David or his kingdom, but this asserted connection with the famous ruler made the site very famous too.

Who were David and Solomon?

There is much more to say about David and Solomon. There are the stories about the fleet that went to collect gold in Ophir, the visit of the Queen of Sheba to Solomon, the relations with the Phoenicians who provided the materials and architects for the building of the temple of Jerusalem. These are amazing stories, but outside of the Bible there is hardly any information covering these events.

So, all in all, external sources that can tell us more about David and Solomon are largely absent. This begs the question of whether these kings actually existed. If so, did they really play a significant role in the political and economic events of the region in those days and did they leave us monumental buildings? So far there is no archaeological evidence to support this. Perhaps, as some scholars suggest, they were local rulers, 'chiefs', whose role in the events of the day was later exaggerated and made more important over time. Is it possible that they have been credited with the brave and noble deeds and the execution of projects that were the work of later kings, such as the building of the temple in Jerusalem, the boosting of international trade, or the rise of urban culture? This kind of reassignment is not unusual in the history of mankind and recalls, for instance, the legends surrounding King Arthur and his Knights of the Round Table.

One thing is clear: in the Bible these two kings represent the Golden Age of ancient Israel. This was a time when the kingdom was united and its kings were strong and shrewd (David) or wise and wealthy (Solomon). They were respected by neighbouring countries and foreign kings came to visit and offered their princesses in marriage. God's benevolent gaze rested on his beloved ones (the name David probably means 'beloved') and He blessed them with prosperity.

Unfortunately, in the history of mankind, Golden Ages have very often proved to be fantasies, figments of the imaginations of either those in power for reasons of their own, or of a people in distress, as a means to hang on to better times, when all that glittered really *was* gold. Such a period, for the people of Israel, was the time of the Exile, when all seemed lost and people looked back longingly to the glory days of the Empire. Whether those glory days ever really existed was of less importance.

The picture of those days painted by archaeology is very different. Current evidence shows the 10th century BC to be a transitional period from a rural society in the Early Iron Age to an urban society in the Late Iron Age, when Israel and Judah at last began to play their part on the world stage, as established political states. Beginning in the 9th century BC we find the names of their kings in Assyrian, Aramaic and Moabite inscriptions, such as the Tel Dan inscription discussed above. In fact, the 'history' of ancient Israel starts in the 9th century BC with the introduction of written sources, whilst the 10th century remains shrouded in mist. If we did not have those beautiful stories about David and Solomon, few historians would be interested in that period.

Chapter 6

In search of ... Jezebel and the House of Omri

Jezebel was the wife of King Ahab of Israel (Fig. 6.1). 1 Kings 16:31 states: 'He ... also married Jezebel daughter of Ethbaal, king of the Sidonians, and began to serve Baal and worship him.' The name Sidonians refers to the Phoenicians. Ethbaal was king of Tyre, the most powerful Phoenician city, so for Ahab an alliance with that city was a shrewd move politically. The queen brought her own gods with her: Baal and Astarte.

With king Ahab and his father king Omri we begin to approach historical times. The history of the kingdoms of Israel and Judah can now be verified using extra-biblical written sources such as inscriptions written on behalf of the kings of Assyria, Moab and Aram (see below). Sometimes the stories written in these annals coincide with the biblical narrative, sometimes they do not – and often the biblical stories deal with different issues than do the inscriptions.

According to the Bible (1 Kings 12–15) after his death in around 930 BC (based on the biblical chronology, see Chapter 5), king Solomon was succeeded by his son Rehoboam. In the course of Rehoboam's reign the kingdom split into the northern kingdom of Israel and the southern kingdom of Judah (Fig. 6.2). In the southern kingdom the descendants of Solomon continued to rule, while in the northern kingdom a sequence of different families usurped the throne, one after another. First Jeroboam, son of Nebat of the tribe of Ephraim, was crowned king of Israel by the northern tribes. His son, Nadab, was murdered by Basah, who then usurped the throne. Next Basah's son Elah was killed by the 'captain of his chariots' Zimri, who wanted to ascend the throne himself. His coup failed, however, because the army proclaimed Omri king of Israel. After a struggle that lasted several years, Omri ascended the throne in *c.* 876 BC. His son Ahab is possibly the most infamous king in the Bible.

For these events, covering a time span of some 55 years, no extra-biblical sources have so far been found that can corroborate them. It is, in fact, not until the reign of king Omri that the historical record becomes tangible. Omri's name appears in inscriptions, particularly Assyrian ones. The Assyrians began to stir in the early 9th century BC, trying to expand their empire in all directions. Their western and southern campaigns brought them into contact with the Aramaeans, Phoenicians and

Figure 6.1 Image of queen Jezebel published by Guillaume Rouille in his book Promptuarium Iconum Insigniorum in the 16th century (public domain).

Israelites, who then formed a coalition in an effort to stop the Assyrian expansion. They succeed – for a while (see below).

Omri's dynasty came to an end when a commander of the army named Jehu murdered king Joram, Omri's grandson. This sorry state of affairs, with kings murdered by aspiring commanders and new families taking over the throne of Israel, was repeated three more times before the Assyrians captured the land in 722 BC and made it into a province of their empire.

In this chapter the history of the northern kingdom of Israel is discussed, focusing on the kings of the Omride dynasty. Towards the end we will return to Jezebel, to see if we can trace her.

Biblical stories

The biblical narrative contains more stories about the elusive kings David and Solomon (mythical or not) than about the historical king Omri, who reigned from 876–869 BC according to the biblical chronology, and about the other kings of his 'house'. The Bible book of Kings remains almost silent on Omri. His reign merits a mere ten verses: 1 Kings 16:16–17 and 21–28. Out of these, five verses describe his ascent to the throne, one the purchase of the hill of Shemer as the location for the new capital, two tell us that he did evil in the eyes of the Lord, and one records his death; finally there is a reference to 'the book of the Chronicles of Israel', that would contain a description of his exploits.

There are several more references to these 'Chronicles of the kings of Israel and Judah' in the Bible. They have not been handed down to us and so we do not know what they contained (or even if they really existed). They may have been court records.

Much more is written about Omri's son king Ahab who reigned 869–850 BC (1 King 16:29–22:40), but that is mostly because of his conflict with the prophet Elijah, a twist described extensively in the verses in question. Ahab was a powerful

Figure 6.2 Map of the kingdoms of the Levant in the Iron Age (Richardprins, Creative Commons Licence CC BY-SA 3.0).

king. According to the Bible he had an ongoing quarrel with the king of Aram, who resided in Damascus and who greedily eyed the wealth of Israel. Together with his ally Judah (Ahab's daughter Athaliah was married to the king of Judah), Ahab fought three wars against Aram. Extra-biblical sources, such as the Tel Dan stele discussed in the previous chapter, confirm this. On the other hand, Ahab also fought side by side with the king of Aram against the Assyrians, something that biblical sources do not mention.

1 King 16:30 says: 'Ahab ... did more to arouse the anger of the Lord, the God of Israel, than did all the kings of Israel before him.' This refers particularly to his religious activities. He married Jezebel, daughter of the king of Tyre. She brought the Phoenician gods Baal and Astarte with her, for whom Ahab built temples and 'heights' in Israel. The story of the struggle between the 70 priests of Baal and the prophet Elijah is hauntingly beautiful (1 Kings 18:20–40).

Ahab was succeeded by his son Ahaziah, who then fell out of the window of his palace in Samaria and was severely wounded. He died shortly afterwards and was succeeded by this brother Joram. After a reign of 12 years, Joram was murdered by his own general, Jehu. The usurpation of the throne by Jehu *c.* 842 BC ends the dynasty of Omri. However, in the Assyrian annals the kingdom of Israel continues to be referred to as the 'house of Omri' and the kings of Israel as the 'sons of Omri'.

The reason that the Bible treats the Omride dynasty (as well as the later kings of Israel) rather disparagingly may lie in the fact that these stories were largely written by scholars and priests of the southern kingdom of Judah. This is likely to have happened just before, during, or just after the Exile (see Chapter 2). These Judaeans would have condemned everything done or achieved by their larger and more prosperous neighbour Israel in the 9th and 8th centuries BC. Thus the destruction of Israel by the Assyrians at the end of the 8th century and the exiling of the 'ten tribes' into Assyria was seen as a just punishment for their sins. This was regardless of the fact that Judah had almost suffered the same fate. However, at the end of the 8th century BC Judah came away unscathed – for the time being – and could look down on its less fortunate neighbours.

Extra-biblical sources

The kings of the House of Omri are mentioned several times in extra-biblical inscriptions, such as the Kurkh Monolith, the Black Obelisk, the Tel Dan inscription and the Mesha Stele.

Kurkh Monolith

In 853 BC a great battle was fought near the Syrian city of Qarqar. For the first time in history the Assyrian expansion was impeded, by a coalition consisting of a large number of kings from countries south and west of Assyria. Troops of the Aramaean king Hadadezer, whose capital was at Damascus, fought side by side with soldiers

Figure 6.3 Detail of Kurkh monolith featuring Shalmaneser III and his deeds (photo: David Castor, public domain).

from a range of Phoenician city states, as well as troops from Arabia and Ammon. The greatest contribution to the battle was made by the Israelite king Ahab who, according to the text, sent a grand total of 2000 chariots and 10,000 soldiers into the battle.

The Bible is silent about this event. Nowhere does it mention that king Ahab fought the Assyrians together with his inveterate enemy, the king of Aram. The battle is, however, recorded in an Assyrian chronicle known as the Kurkh Monolith (Fig. 6.3). The battles from the first six years of the reign of the Assyrian king Shalmaneser III are recorded in detail on this stele. Shalmaneser III reigned 859–824 BC, so these records were inscribed *c.* 850 BC. This stele can now be found in the British Museum.

Of this 'coalition of the willing' it says:

> Karkar, his [that is: Hadadezer's] royal city, I destroyed, I devastated, I burned with fire.
>
> 1,200 chariots, 1,200 cavalry, 20,000 soldiers, of Hadadezer, of Aram;
>
> 700 chariots, 700 cavalry, 10,000 soldiers of Irhulêni of Hamath; 2,000 chariots, 10,000 soldiers of Ahab, the Israelite;
>
> 500 soldiers of the Gueans;
>
> 1,000 soldiers of the Musreans;

> 10 chariots, 10,000 soldiers of the Irkanateans;
> 200 soldiers of Matinuba'il, the Arvadite;
> 200 soldiers of the Usanateans;
> 30 chariots, [ ],000 soldiers of Adunu-ba'il, the Shianean;
> 1,000 camels of Gindibu', the Arabian;
> [ ],000 soldiers [of] Ba'sa, son of Ruhubi, the Ammonite;
> These twelve kings he brought to his support; to offer battle and fight, they came
>   against me.

Note that Judah is not joining the battle, and neither is Moab. Note also that the Assyrian inscription mentions only ten kings that Hadadezer brought to battle with him, not 12 as stated in the last line. Together they form an impressive coalition of 11 kings. That the inscription talks of 12 has puzzled scholars for a long time. It is possible that the Assyrian scribe recording the event forgot to mention one or two of the allies. Another explanation is that the number 12 is symbolic, signifying a full or powerful collation. Shalmaneser does not exactly say that he lost the battle. However, in the years that follow his expansionist aims and ambitions focused mainly on the north and east. It seems that the 11 kings had managed (temporarily) to curb Assyrian progress to the west and south.

Black Obelisk

A later Assyrian campaign against the king of Damascus is described on a large black limestone stele found in Nimrud, the then capital of Assyria, now also in the British Museum. It is dated to around 827 BC and recounts all the campaigns and battles of the king. Here Shalmaneser III describes his battle with king Hazael of Damascus, the successor of Hadadezer, in *c* 840 BC. King Hazael is also mentioned in the Bible.

The relevant part of the inscription says:

> In my eighteenth year, I crossed the Euphrates for the sixteenth time. Hazael of Damascus came out in battle. I captured 1121 of his chariots and 470 of his cavalry from him, along with his camp.

In another Assyrian annal the king recounts this battle against Hazael in greater detail. It says:

> In my eighteenth year, I crossed the Euphrates for the sixteenth time. Hazael of Damascus, trusting in the size of his army, mustered a force of significant size, and established his fortress in Mount Saniru, a mountain peak at the border of Lebanon. I met him in battle, and was able to overthrow him. I killed 6,000 of his soldiers, and apprehended 1,121 of his chariots and 470 of his cavalry, along with his camp. He ran for his life up into the mountain. I followed after him and trapped him in Damascus; his royal city. I cut down his orchards, and advanced as far as Mount Hauran destroying, devastating, and setting fire to countless cities. I carried off a great amount of their spoil. I marched to Mount Ba'li-ra'si, a headland of the [Mediterranean], and set up my royal image there. At that time, I accepted the tribute from the men from Tyre, Sidon, and from Jehu, son of Omri.

It looks as if this time the Aramaeans were on their own. The major Phoenician city-states of Tyre and Sidon, as well as the kingdom of Israel, were already subjugated to the Assyrians, and paid tribute. Once again the Assyrians failed to conquer Damascus. They tried another time, in Shalmaneser's 21st year, but failed again. The Black Obelisk states:

> In my twenty-first year, I crossed the Euphrates for the twenty-first time. I advanced against the cities of Hazael of Syria and captured four of them. I accepted gifts of the Tyrians, Sidonians, and the people of Gebal [Byblos].

The Assyrians captured the main Phoenician cities Tyrus, Sidon and Byblos (Gebal), but obviously not Damascus. They had to wait almost a century, until the campaign of Tiglath-Pileser III in 732 BC, before they succeeded in finally subjugating the Aramean kingdom of Damascus.

Shalmaneser says: 'I set up my royal image there.' 'There' is a narrow pass through the valley of the Nahr el-Kalb (Dog river), north-east of Beirut. In the rocks that flank the pass reliefs have been carved by the many armies that came through: from Egyptian pharaohs and Babylonian kings, down to Napoleon III in 1860. Several of the reliefs belong to Assyrian kings, but they are hard to identify. That one of them was authored by Salmaneser III seems to be beyond doubt.

One of the panels of the Black Obelisk shows a figure kissing the feet of the Assyrian king (to his left) (Fig. 6.4). The heading (in cuneiform) says:

Figure 6.4 Panel of the Black Obelisk showing king Jehu of Israel kneeling before the king of Assyria (photo: Osama Shukir Muhammed Amin, Creative Commons Licence CC BY-SA 4.0).

> Tribute of Jehu, son of Omri. I received from him: silver, gold, a golden bowl, a golden beaker, golden goblets, pitchers of gold, lead, staves for the hand of the king, javelins.

This is the oldest known depiction of an Israelite king, unfortunately for him not in a very flattering pose. Jehu, the usurper, is here called a 'son of Omri'. That is not strictly correct, but likely simply stands for 'king of Israel' (see above).

The Tel Dan Stele

This inscription was more extensively discussed in Chapter 5. It refers to a battle between an unnamed Aramaean king (the deity mentioned is Hadad, supreme deity of the Aramaeans) and the kings of Israel and Judah: Joram and Ahaziah. The events described on the stele probably date to the end of the 9th century BC, which means that the Aramaean king in question must be Hazael. The wars between the kings of Israel and those of Aram/Damascus are described in the Bible in 1 Kings 20–22.

The Mesha Stele

On the Mesha Stele, found in Jordan, king Mesha of Moab describes his war with the kings of Israel, who had occupied Moab. He says:

> Omri was the king of Israel, and he oppressed Moab for many days, for Kemosh was angry with his land. And his son succeeded him, and he said – he too – I will oppress Moab! In my days did he say [so].
> And Omri had taken possession of the whole land of Medeba, and he lived there in his days and half the days of his son, forty years, but Kemosh [resto]red it in my days.

This text is dated around 840 BC or slightly later and will be discussed more extensively in Chapter 7 (see also Fig. 7.1).

With these extra-biblical records we have entered the arena of international politics in which Israel played an important role. The kings of Israel were powerful and respected. They fought against the Arameans and, together with the Arameans and others, against the Assyrians. They conquered Moabite lands and lost them when a powerful king rose up in Moab. Eventually they had to submit to the Assyrian yoke.

Omrid building projects

Unlike Judah, which knew only one capital during the whole of its history, the kingdom of Israel had a number of consecutive capital cities. The fact that Israel experienced a succession of different ruling families may have something to do with this. Each usurping king aimed to create his own capital city, outshining its predecessor. Assyrian kings did the same, although the capital cities of Israel cannot be compared to those of the Assyrians, which were much more impressive and luxurious.

According to the Bible, the old central town of the northern tribes was *Shechem*. Here, long ago, Joshua had made all the tribes swear loyalty to God. Shechem was also the place where the northern tribes seceded and elected Jeroboam as their king (1 Kings 12:1–24), who then chose Shechem as his capital city. Afterwards he left Shechem and reinforced *Pnuel*, on the other side of the Jordan (1 Kings 12:25). The location of Pnuel is not certain. It has repeatedly been suggested that it was at Tell Deir Alla (see Chapter 9). However, no large city dating to the 10th century BC has been found there. King Basah, who had usurped the throne from the son of Jeroboam, made his seat in *Tirzah*, identified with Tell el-Farah (north) (1 Kings 15:25–34).

King Omri wasn't to put up with such a modest residence. According to 1 Kings 16:24: 'He bought the hill of Samaria from Shemer for two talents of silver and built a city on the hill, calling it Samaria, after Shemer, the name of the former owner of the hill.' Ahab expanded and beautified the city. He also founded a second capital: *Jezreel*. But Samaria remained the official capital of the kingdom of Israel until its destruction by the Assyrians in 722 BC.

Samaria was excavated in the 1930s (Fig. 6.5). It is a low mound, the summit of which was occupied by the 'royal quarter'. This consists of a horizontal terrace, some 1.5 ha in size, surrounded by a casemate wall which served both as support wall and to protect the terrace. This wall was 5–10 m wide. Very little is left of the palace itself and a complete reconstruction of its layout is difficult. It consisted of several series of rooms around open courtyards. Other buildings on the terrace yielded interesting finds. Ostraca (sherds with writing on them) were discovered in the floors of building

Figure 6.5 Excavations at Samaria in the 1930s, unearthing Ahab's palace (Matson Photographic Collection, public domain).

Figure 6.6 'Woman at the window' ivory found in the palace of the city of Nimrud in Assyria. Many ivories were found there, which are thought to have come from Samaria as tribute or war spoils (photo: Osama Shukir Muhammed Amin Creative Commons Licence CC BY-SA 4.0).

102, of which 63 were legible. All turned out to be receipts of shipments of wine and olive oil meant for court dignitaries, probably from their own lands.

In another building a large group of ivory inlays was found which once adorned wooden furniture, boxes and cabinets. Most publications give the number of ivory objects as 500. However, recent searches in archives and basements has produced a total number of *c*. 12,000 fragments. The ivory inlays reveal a number of recurrent themes: a winged sphinx, a cow licking her calf, the tree of life, lotus flowers and the 'woman at the window'. This last motif in particular has caught people's attention. It represents a woman's head above a balcony balustrade (Fig. 6.6). It has been linked to the story of queen Jezebel (see below).

The remainder of the city must have been in the area around the royal quarter but unfortunately that area has not been excavated down to the Iron Age levels. The city was in existence from the building of the palace by Omri around 860 BC until the destruction by the Assyrians in 722 BC. The kings of Israel that succeeded Ahab continued to live in his luxurious capital Samaria.

As discussed in Chapter 5, the buildings in Megiddo and Hazor are now dated to the 9th century BC and ascribed to the Omride dynasty. In a recent article Norma Franklin, who has long excavated at Megiddo and is now a director of the new Jezreel excavations, has shown that the palaces of Samaria and of Megiddo were constructed by the same builders. According to her, mason's marks found on some of the building blocks are the same in Megiddo and in Samaria, whilst they differ from those in every other city of that time. The builders also used the same Egyptian cubit, of 45 cm, as a unit of length. Her conclusion is that king Ahab employed the same group of professional masons for his building projects in both Samaria and Megiddo. In later periods, buildings in both cities were constructed in a different style using a different unit of length.

Traces of Queen Jezebel

Jezebel was Ahab's wife. The Bible generally describes Jezebel as a bit of a slut and she is accused of harlotry and witchcraft (2 Kings 9:22). In reality she was the wife, daughter and sister of kings, the mother of two kings and a powerful woman. Her father was Ethbaal, king of Tyre, her brother Baal-Eser I was king of Tyre after him, and her sons Achaziah and Joram succeeded Ahab as king of Israel. Jezebel wrote letters using Ahab's seal (1Kings 21:8), she will have maintained the diplomatic relations with her father, the king of Tyre, and later with her brother who succeeded him, while for king Ahab she was an important and trusted companion.

Jezebel's death is described in the Bible with a fair amount of glee. Her son Joram, the king, was murdered by Jehu, who then proclaimed himself king. 2 Kings 9:30–34 states:

> Then Jehu went to Jezreel. When Jezebel heard about it, she put on eye makeup, arranged her hair and looked out of a window. As Jehu entered the gate, she asked, Have you come in peace, you Zimri, you murderer of your master? He looked up at the window and called out: Who is on my side? Who? Two or three eunuchs looked down at him. Throw her down! Jehu said. So they threw her down, and some of her blood spattered the wall and the horses as they trampled her underfoot.

Interestingly enough, it is Jezebel's painting of her eyes that has invoked the ire of many a preacher down the centuries. A girl with painted eyes was often nicknamed a Jezebel – someone with loose morals. But the biblical stories do not ever mention Jezebel's supposed loose morals. On the contrary, the texts paint her as a dignified and brave woman. She calls the murderer of her son to account, knowing that she will not survive this action. So she makes up her eyes with kohl. The many kohl sticks found in excavations show that, in those days, it was common for women to paint their eyes. Kohl was (and still is) used to ward off evil and as an expression of mourning. Jezebel did not paint her eyes in order to seduce Jehu but to face her death with dignity.

In popular culture Jezebel is definitely in demand. Searching Jezebel in Google Images fills the screen with the most stunning actresses and models. Most telling, in my view, are the two pictures in Figure 6.7. To the left a (to me) unknown actress plays Jezebel. She is depicted as the 'woman at the window' (the ivory on the right) whether on purpose or accidentally. Jezebel is often connected with this motif, because

Figure 6.7 Woman depicted as queen Jezebel (left), and ivory 'women at the window' (right, public domain).

of the biblical text mentioned above: she looked out of the window. She probably stood on the balcony looking down. Perhaps women were expected to stay indoors and balconies had the same function as they have today in traditional Arab houses: to give women the opportunity to look outside without being seen. Or perhaps we are now starting to read a bit too much in the 'balcony theme'.

Jezebel's seal?

In recent years there has been some debate over a seal that may bear the name of queen Jezebel (Fig. 6.8). The seal comes from a private collection that was donated to the Israeli Antiquities Authority in the 1960s and published in 1964 by Nahman Avigad. He identified the name Jezebel on the seal, but stopped short of saying that this was, therefore, queen Jezebel's seal – even though the stone was worthy of a queen while Jezebel is not a very common Phoenician name. One argument against identifying the seal with 'our' Jezebel is that the name on the seal is spelled slightly differently from the biblical spelling.

In 2007 Marjo Korpel, from Utrecht University in the Netherlands, published an article that argued for identification of the seal as that of the famous queen. As usual, not everybody agrees with her. As shown in Figure 6.8, it is a beautiful seal stone, 'fit for a queen' (which is also the title of Korper's article). There is a winged sphinx at the top, above a winged sun over a falcon, three symbols of royalty in ancient Egypt.

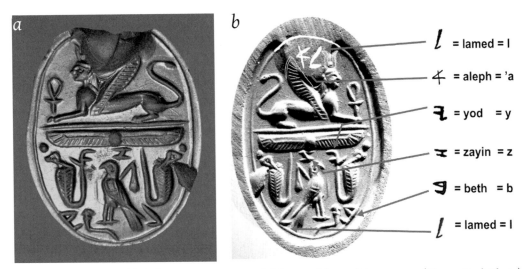

Figure 6.8 a. Seal, possibly belonging to queen Jezebel (www.BibleLandPictures.com/Alamy Stock Photo). b. Seal of Jezebel (Courtesy Marjo Korpel).

The sphinx is said to wear a Hathor-wig, signifying that the owner of the seal was a woman. Phoenicians often used Egyptian symbolism.

What is strange, however, is that the characters of the name are scattered across the stone. This gives the impression that the seal was originally made for a queen without a name inscribed, and that the letters of the name were crammed into the image at a later stage. That may suggest a forgery, although not necessarily so. Perhaps it was an existing seal, which Jezebel saw and liked so much that she wanted it as her official seal stone. The fact that she had her own seal would confirm that she was a powerful woman, whose official correspondence had to be sealed with her own name. This is the only extra-biblical source that carries the name Jezebel.

The House of Omri

As discussed, the written history of Israel begins with king Omri. He is the first king mentioned as such in an extra-biblical source (the Mesha Stele) and he brought stability and wealth to the northern kingdom. For centuries to come the Assyrians would call the kingdom of Israel the 'House of Omri' and its kings 'sons of Omri', irrespective of any family relationship. His son Ahab was one of the kings in the coalition fighting off the Assyrian threat, as described in the Kurkh Stele.

The biblical and extra-biblical sources do not always completely coincide. Most conspicuous is the absence of any allusion in the biblical verses to the battle Ahab fought against the Assyrians, together with his eternal foe the king of Damascus and other allies. However, both inscriptions and biblical texts agree that Ahab was a mighty king.

Ahab's wife Jezebel generally gets a bad press in the biblical narrative and is not mentioned in any written historical records, though she may have been a powerful woman in her own right. Whether the seal with the name Jezebel really belonged to the queen remains uncertain.

Chapter 7

In search of ... Mesha of Moab

According to the Bible, Mesha of Moab was an enemy of Israel against whom several wars were fought. The Bible is derogatory and calls him 'a sheep breeder'. But, by his own account, he was a powerful ruler who chased the king of Israel out of his territory. This account is written on a large inscribed stone stele, found in Transjordan in the 19th century (Fig. 7.1).

In this chapter the various theories about Mesha, biblical and otherwise, will be discussed as well as several excavations in Moab. The chapter concludes with an excursus on the discovery of the stele.

The land of Moab

In the 9th and 8th centuries BC when the House of Omri ruled in Israel (Chapter 6), a new dynasty emerged on the other side of the Jordan: that of Moab. The biblical text is not very specific about events there, and the Assyrians were not very interested either, so there are but few inscriptions mentioning Moab. This lack of interest was reflected in the state of archaeological research in Moab, which likewise lagged behind for a long time. Fortunately, we now know much more about Moab and its great king Mesha.

Iron Age Transjordan can be divided into five separate areas (see Fig. 6.2). Opposite the kingdom of Israel is the region of Gilead, consisting of the northern Jordan valley and the hill country to the east. According to the Bible, Gilead was once part of Israel and inhabited by the tribes of Gad, Ruben and Manasseh. In the hill country to the east of Gilead was the kingdom of Ammon. To the south of Ammon was Moab and, in the far south, Edom. The most northern part of the land belonged to the kingdom of Aram-Damascus.

In those days the borders between kingdoms or regions were not fixed. There were no maps on which borders could be outlined, nor barbed wire with which they could be demarcated. The usual way to discern one country from another was by means of the location of its towns. Towns belonged to a kingdom, together with the surrounding countryside with its grain, olives, grapes and wood. Wars were fought to control these towns and the fertile regions they managed. The uninhabited countryside in between

Figure 7.1 Mesha Stele (Louvre Museum, Creative Commons Licence CC BY 3.0).

Figure 7.2 Ancient Moab with the Wadi Mujib (biblical Arnon), cutting a deep ravine through the landscape (photo: David Bivin).

served as thoroughfare and was the territory of roaming nomads. Often the peoples of Israel or Moab identified themselves with the tribe of which they were part, rather than with the kingdom to which their territory happened to belong to at a certain moment.

Moab was a fertile region, consisting of hills and plains, cut through by several east–west flowing rivers discharging into the Dead Sea (Fig. 7.2). Over time, these rivers had cut deep ravines into the landscape. The land of Moab was partly arable land that abounded in corn and partly pasture with sheep grazing on it. We will meet the Moabite flocks of sheep further on.

Moab in the Bible

The Moabites are traditionally seen as the descendants of one of the sons of Lot, called Moab. The other son was Ben-Ammi, the ancestor of the Ammonites. The fascinating tale of their conception is written in Genesis 19:30–38. Although, according to this story, the Moabites were related to the Israelites (which are the descendants of Abraham who was Lot's uncle), they are commonly depicted as one of the principal enemies of Israel, and real baddies. When the Israelites, after 40 years of wandering

Figure 7.3 Ruth in Boaz' Field by Julius Schnorr von Carolsfeld (1794-1872) (National Gallery London, public domain).

in the desert, finally marched towards the Promised Land, they were stopped by the king of Moab. The prophet Balaam had to come to the rescue to help them take that hurdle (see Chapter 9).

The most famous Moabite in the Bible is certainly Ruth (Fig. 7.3). Her story can be found in the book carrying her name. She is the daughter-in-law of Naomi who, with her family, emigrated from Judah during a famine and settled in Moab. After the death of all the menfolk in the family Naomi wants to return to her home country of Judah. Ruth, the Moabite, goes with her, speaking the famous words: 'Where you go I will go, and where you stay I will stay. Your people will be my people and your God my God.' (Ruth 1:16).

In the biblical narrative she becomes the paragon of faithfulness and loyalty, but also of cunning and the power of sexuality. Read how she seduces the wealthy landowner Boaz (in Ruth 3). It is a beautiful story, one that returns repeatedly in modern literature. Ruth becomes one of the ancestors of the great king David which would mean that he had Moabite roots.

Moab outside of the Bible

Moab is briefly mentioned in Neo-Assyrian inscriptions such as that of Tiglath-Pileser III who reigned 745–727 BC. This inscription states that the kings of Ammon, Edom and Moab paid tribute to the Assyrian king, as a token of submission. On the other hand, the Kurkh monolith and the Black Obelisk, both from the 9th century BC, don't mention Moab at all (see chapter 6). It wasn't until the 8th century BC that the Assyrians saw the region as an important transit route for incense and other Arabian goods.

The Mesha Stele

Fortunately a large inscription was found in Moab itself, commissioned by king Mesha, who is mentioned in the Bible (Figs 7.1 and 7.4). The discovery of the stone, and the commotion it triggered, are described later in this chapter. The stele is dated to the second half of the 9th century BC, around 840 or 830 BC.

The text begins as follows:

> I am Mesha, the son of Kemosh[-yatti], the king of Moab, the Dibonite. My father was king over Moab for thirty years, and I was king after my father. And I made this high-place for Kemosh in Qarcho ... because he has delivered me from all kings, and because he has made me look down on all my enemies.
> Omri was the king of Israel, and he oppressed Moab for many days, for Kemosh was angry with his land. And his son succeeded him, and he said – he too – I will oppress Moab! In my days did he say [so].
> And Omri had taken possession of the whole land of Medeba, and he lived there in his days and half the days of his son, forty years. But Kemosh [resto]red it in my days.

So Mesha states that Omri, king of Israel, had incorporated parts of northern Moab in his kingdom, that is the region around Madaba, but when his son became king, Mesha took back the land with the help of the his deity Kemosh, for whom he had built a sanctuary in Qarcho (possibly the capital Dhiban).

Next Mesha elaborates on his building projects and his heroic war record:

> And I built Baal Meon, and I made in it a water reservoir, and I built Qiryaten. And the men of Gad lived in the land of Atarot, from ancient times; and the king of Israel built Atarot for himself, and I fought against the city and captured it, and I killed all the people [from] the city as a sacrifice for Kemosh and for Moab.

Mesha recounts in detail how he captured of the towns of Nebo and Jahaz from the Israelites, after he has conscripted 200 'men' (war leaders?) from Moab.

> And Kemosh said to me: Go, take Nebo from Israel. And I went in the night and I fought against it from the break of dawn until noon, and I took it and I killed [its] whole population: seven thousand male citizens and aliens, and female citizen and aliens, and servant girls; for I had put it to the ban for Ashtar Kemosh. And from there I took th[e ves]sels of Yahweh, and I hauled them before the face of Kemosh.

Figure 7.4 Drawing of Mesha inscription (Mark Lidzbarski, published 1898, public domain).

Follows another summing up of building projects:

> I have built Qarcho, the wall of the woods and the wall of the citadel, and I have built
> its gates, and I have built its towers, and I have built the house of the king, and I have
> made the double reser[voir for the spr]ing in the innermost part of the city, in Qarcho.
> And I cut the moat for Qarcho by means of prisoners from Israel. I have built Aroer, and
> I made the military road in the Arnon. I have built Beth Bamot, for it was destroyed. I
> have built Bezer, for [it lay in] ruins.

The ending is unclear, because that part of the stone is missing.

The Mesha Stele has been of major importance for the study of ancient languages and linguistics for biblical scholarship and for the history and archaeology of the region. The text provides us with information on the kingdom of Moab and its towns, such as Madaba, Atarot, Jahaz, Dhiban, Nebo and Aroer. Mesha talks exclusively about the northern part of his country with its capital Dhiban/Dibon, while the biblical stories on Moab seem to focus largely on the southern part of Moab and the capital Kir Hareset (Kerak), Some scholars therefore believe that Kir Hareset is not Kerak but Karcho or Qarch, which probably is Dhiban.

The inscription also provides insight into the history of Moab's struggle with the Israelites (and, as a consequence, into the history of Israel), into the political relations of the period, and into the economy and the religion of the Moabites. It also is the first extra-biblical source that mentions the name of Israel's god, YHWH: 'And from there I took Yahweh's vessels, and I presented them before Kemosh's face.' This obviously means that there was a temple dedicated to YHWH in Nebo, and Mesha robbed it of its inventory and brought this to the temple of Kemosh in Dhiban, which was the ultimate shame.

According to the French epigraphist André Lemaire the words 'House of David' appear twice in the inscription. To get there, he had to insert some missing characters. As in the Tel Dan inscription (discussed in Chapter 5), the words 'House of David' are interpreted to mean the kingdom of Judah. If Lemaire is right that would support the Tel Dan inscription, which dates from roughly the same period. As usual, not everybody agrees with this reading.

Who was king Mesha?

Apart from the inscription, we only know king Mesha from a couple of biblical texts. 2 Kings 3:4–27 tells about an expedition which king Joram or Jehoram of Israel undertook against Moab, together with king Josaphat of Judah and an unnamed king of Edom.

The narrative starts like this:

> Now Mesha king of Moab raised sheep, and he had to pay the king of Israel a tribute
> of a hundred thousand lambs and the wool of a hundred thousand rams. But after
> Ahab died, the king of Moab rebelled against the king of Israel. So at that time King

> Joram set out from Samaria and mobilized all Israel. He also sent this message to
> Jehoshaphat king of Judah: The king of Moab has rebelled against me. Will you go with
> me to fight against Moab? I will go with you, he replied. I am as you are, my people as
> your people, my horses as your horses.

After a long journey and several run-ins with the prophet Elisha, the king of Israel
came face to face with the enemy, and the two armies clashed. The Israelites pursued
the Moabites well into their own homeland and defeated them. They destroyed cities,
spoiled fertile fields with stones, stopped up the springs and wells and cut down
every fruit tree. In the end only the city of Kir Hareset remained standing but then
the Israelite stone-slingers surrounded the city and started slinging stones at it.

The king of Moab realised that he was losing the battle and, together with 700
of his most experienced warriors, he tried to escape to the king of Edom, but failed.
Then he took his eldest son, the heir to the throne, and sacrificed him as a burnt
offering on the city wall. That gesture so horrified the Israelites that they abandoned
the attack and returned home.

This biblical text demonstrates that for a while Moab was indeed subjected to
Israelite rule, just as the Mesha Stele states. Moab had to pay a yearly tribute of lambs
(for meat) and unshorn rams (for wool). But after the death of king Ahab, Mesha
jumps at the chance and revolts. Joram, the new king of Israel, together with his
allies attacks Moab but apparently fails to bring it back into line. The Bible blames
his failure on the 'abhorrent' deed of Mesha, the sacrifice of his eldest son: terrified
and disgusted, the Israelites, Judeans and Edomites returned to their home countries.
In most biblical stories where armies leave the battlefield because they are shocked
or because an angel appears, this camouflages a defeat: no, we were not defeated, we
simply had to go home. Assyrian inscriptions do the same.

The events described in the book of Kings are to a large extent confirmed by the
Mesha inscription. Mesha is the rightful king of Moab, the successor of his father
Kemosh-yatti, who was king of Moab before him. Mesha confirms that Moab was
subject to Israelite rule but he rebels and succeeds in expelling the Israelites from his
land – not, as the Bible suggests, by sacrificing his son, but (according to the inscription)
by attacking and reconquering each city in turn and expelling the Israelites.

The two sources differ mainly in the time frame they describe. According to the
inscription, Mesha's rebellion takes place halfway into the reign of the son of Omri,
who had subjected Moab. That son is Ahab, which means that the rebellion would
have taken place around 860 BC according to the biblical chronology. According to
the Bible, however, the rebellion took place after Ahab's death, so after 853 BC.

Klaas Smelik thinks it is unlikely that Mesha would have succeeded in throwing
off the Israelite yoke during Ahab's reign. Ahab was simply too powerful a king, and
according to the Assyrian sources (see Chapter 6) he had a strong army. Ahab was
succeeded by his son Ahaziah, who fell out of the window of his palace in Samaria and
died of his wounds shortly afterwards. He was succeeded by his brother Joram, who
did not wait but set out to suppress the Moabite rebellion. Both sources, the Bible and

the Mesha stele, agree that he failed to do so although they differ (understandably) in the reasons they give for that failure.

It is possible that the Mesha Stele talks about the son of Omri in the same way the Assyrian inscriptions talk about 'son of Omri': to denote the king of Israel, irrespective of whether said king really was a son, a grandson or had no relationship at all.

The name of Mesha also appears on two smaller inscriptions found in Moab. The first is a stone fragment from the Moabite capital of Dhiban, with a reference to 'The House of [Ke]mos' (possibly a temple). A larger fragment, found in Kerak, may mention the name of Mesha's father, Kemosh-yat, but this is not completely certain.

Excavations in Moab

The first excavations in Moab were conducted in the 1950s at Dhiban. More large-scale excavations in the region began in the 1990s, in Madaba, Mudayna Thamad, Ataruz (Atarot) and Mudaybi. The excavations at Dhiban and Mudayna Thamad will be discussed below, while the temple excavated in Ataruz will be examined later in the chapter.

Dhiban

The Mesha Stele was found near the town that, according to the Bible, was the capital of Moab: Dhiban or Dibon. In the stele, king Mesha calls himself 'the Dhibanite', the man from Dhiban. It is not surprising therefore, that the first large-scale expedition in Jordan was the excavation of Mesha's Dhiban.

The work started in the 1950s, directed by American archaeologists. Unfortunately they could not expose much of the Iron Age town because the Romans had thoroughly removed the ancient remains when they built their new town there. However, much Iron Age pottery was found in the massive rubble and foundation layers, some of which had a depth of up to 11 m.

The conclusion of the excavators was that in Iron Age IIB (late 9th–early 8th century BC), the original area of the town was expanded by *c.* 0.75 ha, reaching a total extent of about 3 ha. That does not sound like much, but a lot of effort was put into this expansion which the excavators attributed to king Mesha (who else?). The archaeologists also found several tombs, hewn into bedrock and dating to the Iron Age. Three of these were still replete with funeral gifts, such as pottery bowls and jars, jewellery and cylinder seals.

A new series of excavations started at Dhiban in 2004, on a more modest scale, conducted by the Jordanian Department of Antiquities, together with an international excavation team.

Mudayna Thamad

Mudayna Thamad is an important settlement dated to the Iron IIB/C period (9th–7th centuries BC). It overlooks the Wadi ath-Thamad, on the northern border of ancient

Figure 7.5 Aerial photograph of Mudayna Thamad (photo: Robert Bewley (APAAME_2018014_RHB-0026). Aerial Photographic Archive of Archaeology in the Middle East).

Moab (Fig. 7.5). The site has been excavated since 1996 by Wilfred Laurier University, Canada. Some fascinating discoveries have been made during the excavation. The settlement is defended by a casemate wall which, in its turn, is surrounded by a dry moat. The town is entered through a six-chambered gate. Behind the gate was an open square with a small temple (about which more below). A road led from the square into the city past several pillared buildings. Similar gates, casemate walls and pillared buildings have been found in Megiddo and Hazor in Israel (Chapter 5).

In recent years a fierce debate has flared up about the identification of Mudayna Thamad. With which town, mentioned either in the Bible or on the Mesha Stele, should Mudayna be equated? Every town that is mentioned on the Mesha Stele has been identified with one of the tell sites in northern Moab, except Jahaz. The inscription says: 'And the king of Israel had built Jahaz, and he stayed there throughout his campaign against me; and Kemosh drove him away before my face.'

Jahaz must be located somewhere in northern Moab, close to Dhiban and Madaba. It must also have been a substantial town. Mudayna is one of the few sites that answers that description. Israel Finkelstein has written an article in which he equates Mudayna with Jahaz and suggests that Mudayna was built by king Omri of Israel. As evidence he states the presence of the casemate wall, six-chambered gate and pillared buildings, as this combination also occurs in Megiddo and Hazor (Chapter 5). These buildings have long been dated to the 10th century BC and attributed to king Solomon, but in the 'low chronology' they are dated to the 9th century, and attributed to king Omri.

The excavator of Mudayna Thamad, Michele Daviau, is unconvinced by the identification of her site with Jahaz, or the attribution to king Omri. She has some sound arguments. The pottery that has been excavated from the site looks nothing like that found in Israel: it is clearly Moabite. The few seals and inscriptions that have been found, such as the inscription on the incense altar discussed below, are written in Moabite script and language, both of which differ somewhat from Hebrew script and language.

So who is right here? I think both Finkelstein and Daviau have a point. They are in fact talking of different issues. Finkelstein refers to the time that Mudayna was built which can be dated in the 9th century BC on the basis of radiocarbon samples. In those days it was a small town, with a six-chambered gate, a casemate wall and pillared buildings, just like Megiddo and Hazor. However, the archaeological evidence cannot tell us which king was the builder of that town. Towns and cities are built by architects and craftsmen, not by kings, at least not directly. It is possible that various kings in the area used the same architects who built identical gates, or that different architects copied each others' buildings because they liked them, or because they were practical.

Daviau's conclusion that Mudayna is clearly Moabite, on the other hand, is based on the finds from the last phase of the town's occupation just before it was destroyed, possibly by the Babylonians around 600 BC or possibly somewhat earlier by an unknown enemy – the pottery cannot easily be dated within a century. Pottery, inscriptions and seals from that phase all point to Moabite inhabitants of the town which is to be expected because, by then, Mudayna was located in an area where no Israelites lived anymore.

The evidence at Mudayna Thamad suggests two possible scenarios. Either the town was built by Israelites and later conquered by Moabites or it was built by Moabites, possibly conquered by Israelites (according to the Mesha Stele) and later retaken by Mesha. The style of the buildings cannot determine which scenario is the most plausible and neither can the pottery.

So is Mudayna Jahaz? Possibly, but it would be helpful if we found some evidence to support this identification. Was Mudayna built by Israelites? Maybe yes, maybe no. Finally, were Moabites living in Mudayna? Yes, absolutely. But that is the only certainty we have.

Moab's religion

The religion of the Moabites, as presented in the Mesha Stele, shows that it was rather similar to the religion of Ancient Israel as described in the Bible. To name a few things in common: the king has been put on his throne and is protected by the deity; Success in war is dependent on the deity's moods: a bad temper is fatal for the king's success, however, if the deity is in a good mood, the war is won; the deity's temper is, in turn, determined by the behaviour of the king and his people. Building a temple for the god is always a wise move.

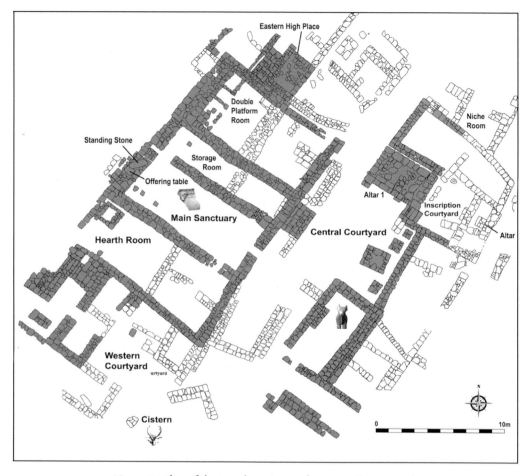

Figure 7.6 Plan of the temple at Ataruz (courtesy Chang-Ho Ji).

A conquered city is 'put to the ban' or 'devoted to the Lord', terms also mentioned in the Bible (see for example Joshua 6:17). It is not entirely clear what 'put to the ban' means but it always results in the extermination of the entire population of the town, as happened at Jericho. Furthermore, the king builds sanctuaries for the local deity and drags important sacred objects from the temple of a conquered town to his own temple, as did the Philistines with the Ark of the Covenant (1 Samuel 4:11). In effect, it looks as if the essential difference between the religions of Israel and Moab lies in the name of the supreme deity: Kemosh versus YHWH.

Temples

A number of temples and smaller shrines have been excavated in Moab. In *Khirbet Ataruz* (Atarot in the Mesha Stele), close to the Dead Sea, a large building has been excavated in recent years and interpreted as a temple (Fig. 7.6). It consists of three

Figure 7.7 Cult stand found in the temple at Ataruz, featuring two male figures in the door opening of a building (photo: Margreet Steiner).

parallel rooms, in which a large number of unusual objects have been found, such as an 'architectural model', which represents a house or temple, with two male figures standing in the doorway (Fig. 7.7).

The excavator, Chang-Ho Ji, dates the building to the 10th century BC – largely because of the Mesha Stele. Ji assumes that Ataruz was an Israelite town that was destroyed by king Mesha, just as the Mesha stele describes, which event must, therefore, have taken place around 840 BC. The temple was also destroyed in that attack. As it has several building phases which means that it was in use for a long time so it 'therefore' must have been built in the 10th century by (who else?) King Solomon. That would make the temple of Ataruz the first and oldest Israelite temple ever excavated.

Ji assumes that Ataruz was not reoccupied after its destruction so that the ruins of the temple which he excavated must have been the result of Mesha's attack. However, Ji's dating is contentious. First, the town itself has not been excavated so we do not know if it was ever attacked and, if so, whether it was rebuilt again, including the temple. Secondly, Ji does not entirely base his dates on pottery. The finds in the temple date it to the Late Iron Age (10th–6th century BC) but there is no particular reason to date it so early in that period. The temple could just have well functioned

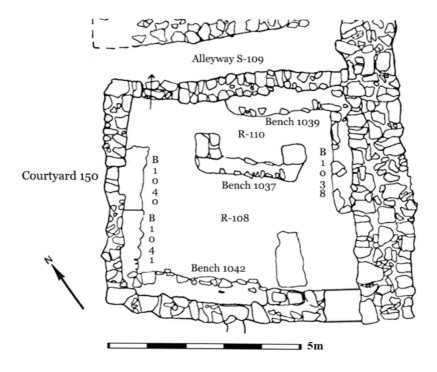

Courtyard 150

Alleyway S-109

Bench 1039

R-110

Bench 1037

R-108

Bench 1042

5m

Figure 7.8 Plan of the small temple at Mudayna Thamad (courtesy Wadi ath-Thamd Project).

in the 9th or 8th centuries BC. A later date, however, would make it a Moabite temple instead of an Israelite one. So, we must wait for the final publication of the finds and the pottery: the jury is still out on this.

Another temple has been excavated in the town of *Mudayna Thamad*, discussed above. This sanctuary is much smaller than that of Ataruz and can be dated to the 8th or 7th century BC. It consists of a square building, measuring *c.* 8 × 8 m, with benches against the inner walls (Fig. 7.8). These were not meant to sit on but were the repositories for gifts to the deity. A number of incense altars were found here, one of which had an inscription, which reads: 'The incense altar that Elishama made for YSP, the daughter of 'WT' (Fig. 7.9). This is the first occurrence of the words 'incense altar' on an actual incense altar so we know for certain what it is. Not much else was found in this temple to give a clue as to which deity it was dedicated.

Mesha searched for and found

We were on a search for king Mesha of Moab, who is mentioned in the Bible as the enemy of the kings of Israel. Have we found him? Certainly. There is a lot of information on him on the Mesha Stele. Mesha succeeded his father as king of Moab, had his capital in Dhiban, went to war with the Israelites over control of northern Moab, and won the battles over the towns of Nebo, Jahaz and Ataruz, thus consolidating his kingdom. He built sanctuaries for his god Kemosh and executed other building projects with the help of Israelite prisoners of war. The excavation projects in Moab have increased our knowledge considerably but much is still unpublished. So far it seems that the results largely confirm the claims of Mesha's inscription.

The discovery of the Mesha Stele

It seems so easy: a stele has been discovered with an important inscription, several scholarly publications explain the ins and outs of the text, it is exhibited in a major museum and thousands of visitors come to see it every year.

But most finds visible in museums have a long and laborious record of discovery and retrieval before they end up on a shelf somewhere. The Mesha Stele has an exceptionally chequered history which is closely connected to the political situation in Palestine at the time, where the major European powers were trying to get a foothold, and to the newly established archaeological museums in Berlin, London and Paris.

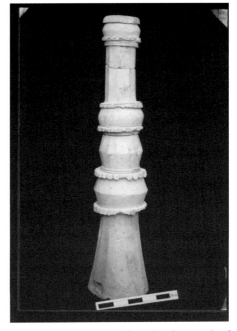

Figure 7.9 Incense stand found in the temple of Mudayna Thamad with an inscription (photo: Margreet Steiner).

Discovery

At the end of the summer of 1868 two horsemen are travelling through the wild countryside east of the Dead Sea. One is Shattam, son of the sheikh of the Bedouin tribe of Beni Sakhr. He is the guide and protector of Dr F. A. Klein, a missionary travelling through the biblical Land of Moab with the aim to convert the locals to Christianity. Travel in these areas is a dangerous undertaking in the 19th century. Officially the lands east of the Jordan are part of the great Ottoman Empire but in reality the Sultan has little power or influence there and the region is controlled by Bedouin tribes. They fight the Sultan's soldiers, as well as each other, attack and rob towns and villages and harass travellers in their territory. The main tribes are the Adwani, the Beni Sakhr and the Beni Hamida (Fig. 7.10). Klein, in order to travel safely, needs the protection of a local guide and must contact the sheikhs that control the territory through which he travels and pay protection money to each of them.

Figure 7.10 Group of young Bedouin women of the Adwan tribe in the beginning of the 20th century (Matson Photographic Collection, public domain).

On August 19, Klein and Shattam are the guests of a Beni Hamida sheikh who has pitched his tents near Dhiban, once the capital of the kingdom of Moab but now a deserted heap of ruins. While they are sipping their ritual cup of Bedouin coffee the sheikh mentions a large stone with an inscription which he has never before shown to any western visitor. He offers to take Klein and Shattam to see the stone.

Klein jumps at the opportunity. He describes the stone in his diary: a large basalt stone with 34 lines of text, lying flat on the ground with the inscription facing upwards. He has the stone turned over to see if there is more on the other side – taking the strength of four men – but the back side of the stone is blank. Although Klein is no expert in ancient languages, he immediately realises the importance of the stone. He copies a few words to show experts in Jerusalem so they can determine the language of the inscription.

What follows is a sequence of misunderstandings and missed opportunities against the background of the growing interest of the western powers in the Levant, particularly Britain, France and Prussia. Klein is a German-speaking Prussian, raised in (French) Strasbourg and employed by the Anglican Church Missionary Society.

He reports his discovery of the stone to the Prussian consul in Jerusalem who is also a student of Semitic languages. The consul studies the copy which Klein has made of part of the inscription and concludes that it must be 'Phoenician'. He immediately contacts the Royal Museum in Berlin and asks whether they are interested in acquiring the stone and are willing to pay for it. After two weeks he receives a commitment for 100 golden Napoleons and he starts negotiations with the Beni Hamida through Klein, who writes a letter to the sheikh.

Imprint

In the meantime both the French and the British in Jerusalem have heard of Klein's discovery of an important inscription. In particular, Charles Clermont-Ganneau, an orientalist who works at the French consulate as a translator, and Charles Warren of the Palestine Exploration Fund (PEF) show a keen interest. However, in diplomatic circles it is not done to interfere while the Prussians are still negotiating. So Warren only reports the find to the PEF and asks for money for a possible purchase of the stone in case the Prussian negotiations come to nothing. He receives no reply. Clermont-Ganneau, who will claim afterwards that he already knew about the existence of the stone and therefore is the true discoverer, is incensed at the idea that this inscription is lying there in the wilderness while no copies or imprints have been made. What if something happens to it? Behind the back of the Prussian negotiators he sends three Arabs with special paper and money to Dhiban to arrange with the local Bedouin to make an imprint of the inscription.

Letters that have been carved in stone can be difficult to read. Such a stone is often covered in dirt, its surface time-worn, with grooves and cracks that look like characters. The tried and tested method for making copies was to cover the stone with wet papier-mâché, press it down well with a brush and let it dry. The result is a negative of the inscription: what is incised in the original, shows up as ridges in the copy. These copies were sometimes easier to read than the original. It is a method that is still in use today.

The three Arabs (who are the heroes in this story) are received hospitably by the Beni Hamida and obtain permission to make an imprint. Unfortunately, while they are working, a violent fight breaks out among the tribe members themselves and the three men jump on their horses and flee. One of them, Sheikh Jamil, manages to dive into the pit in which the stone lies, grabs the drying imprint, and crams it into his coat pocket, after which he escapes by the skin of his teeth, thus securing the only existing complete (although crumpled and occasionally unreadable) copy of the stone. Back in Jerusalem Clermont-Ganneau is disappointed with the result of the expedition but he begins the labour of deciphering and translating the inscription.

Letter from the Sultan

In the meantime, the Prussian negotiations are stalling. The (new) Prussian consul has reached an agreement with the Beni Hamida about the purchase of the ston, and he has sent his men, with the money, to Moab. But now the Adwani are obstructing. The Beni Hamida will have to transport the stone through Adwani territory but no permission is given. The reason is not entirely clear, but it is likely that the Beni Hamida do not want to pay (enough) protection money. Negotiations, as well as the stone itself, have come to a complete standstill.

But then help comes from high up. The Prussians have used official diplomatic channels in Istanbul and requested permission from the Sultan himself to buy the stone. A letter arrives from the Sublime Porte, addressed to the Pasha of Jerusalem, granting official permission for the purchase of the stone and ordering the local authority to assist the Prussians in their purchase of it. Unfortunately the Pasha of Jerusalem has nothing to do with Moab. The Pasha of Nablus is the one with authority in Moab but he is subordinate to the Wali of Damascus. Therefore the letter from the sultan needs to go to Damascus first, to finally arrive in Nablus. The Pasha of Nablus lets it be known that he is prepared to send soldiers to the Beni Hamida to force them to hand over the stone – which they were willing to do anyway. By now it has been a year since Klein saw the stone for the first time.

Tragedy

We are now reaching the dramatic climax of the story. At the end of 1869, when everything finally seems set for a happy ending, news reaches Jerusalem that the stone has been smashed to pieces. The Beni Hamida have lighted a fire underneath and then poured cold water over it. The pieces have been divided among the tribe members who have placed them in their beds and stables as a powerful charm to increase fertility.

It has never become clear why the Beni Hamida destroyed the stone. Several explanations have been suggested. One is that the interest of western diplomats made them realise that the stone was valuable. To them that meant that it contained gold and so they broke it up to get at the gold inside. Another explanation is that the Beni Hamida resented the interference of the Ottoman authorities in the negotiations. Bedouin never tolerated government interference in their affairs and there had been several recent skirmishes with the Ottoman army. The mere suggestion that the Ottoman army could force them to hand over the stone may have been enough for them to smash it to pieces.

Epilogue

With the destruction and disappearance of the stone, the Prussians lose interest, while Clermont-Ganneau and Warren try to buy as many fragments as possible from the Bedouin. Unbeknown to each other, they both send some trusted local men to Dhiban to make imprints of the fragments that are still lying about. The two teams meet halfway and decide to work together on the imprints. At that time, Warren is still waiting for a response to his letters to the PEF and his requests for money to purchase the stone. Altogether he sends five letters before he finally gets a response, in March 1870. The contents of the response shock him deeply. The PEF congratulates him with the discovery of the stone and demands to know why he hesitated so long before buying it, why he smashed it, and why he handed over his imprints to Clermont-Ganneau – a plethora of misunderstanding. Warren writes one more letter, to explain and rehabilitate himself, and then resigns from his job.

In the other camp, Clermont-Ganneau is still busy collecting fragments of the stone. By now the Bedouin themselves are making imprints of pieces. They offer him these pieces for sale, including the imprints. In a letter he writes that in this way altogether about 60% of the stone has been recovered. Later in that year he publishes the first version of his translation of the text. The fragments are transported to the Louvre in Paris, where the stone is being restored and exhibited. It is still one of the major showpieces of the museum.

Chapter 8

In search of ... Jehoiachin and the Exile

Let us turn our attention to a king who sat on the throne of Judah for a very short time but during which he saw Jerusalem attacked by the armies of the mighty Neo-Babylonian king Nebuchadnezzar II, was dethroned and (with many of his fellow Judeans) sent into exile to Babylonia. He survived the gruelling journey and spent dozens of years in a prison, only to be miraculously released and ended his life as the esteemed guest of the king of Babylon, dining at his table. How do we know all this? Because biblical texts and Babylonian cuneiform inscriptions both tell part of his same story and, for once, they do not contradict each other too much. The story of king Jehoiachin, who reigned in Jerusalem for three months at the end of 598 and the beginning of 597 BC, is part of the narrative of the end of the Judaean kingdom and the sad story of the Exile (Fig. 8.1).

Jehoiachin in biblical texts

After his father Jehoiachim (with an 'm') had been killed by raiders, Jehoiachin (with an 'n') became king of the small vassal state of Judah. He was only 18 years old. Although the kingdom was subjugated to the great empire of Babylonia, his father had sided with Egypt in a rebellion against Babylon. The Babylonian king Nebuchadnezzar II would have none of it. He campaigned against Egypt and defeated it and a few years later he marched through Judah and besieged Jerusalem, just as Jehoiachin had ascended the throne.

2 Kings 24: 12–15 states:

> In the eighth year of the reign of the king of Babylon, he took Jehoiachin prisoner. As the Lord had declared, Nebuchadnezzar removed the treasures from the temple of the Lord and from the royal palace, and cut up the gold articles that Solomon king of Israel had made for the temple of the Lord. He carried all Jerusalem into exile: all the officers and fighting men, and all the skilled workers and artisans—a total of ten thousand. Only the poorest people of the land were left. Nebuchadnezzar took Jehoiachin captive to Babylon. He also took from Jerusalem to Babylon the king's mother, his wives, his officials and the prominent people of the land.

Figure 8.1 Image of king Jehoiachin published by Guillaume Rouille in his book Promptuarium Iconum Insigniorum in the 16th century (public domain).

So not only the king was sent away, but his household, nobles, officers and craftsmen as well. The temple, which doubled as the treasury of the state, was plundered. Nebuchadnezzar installed Jehoiachin's uncle, Zedekiah, on the throne. Surprisingly after the disaster of 597 BC, just ten years later Zedekiah rebelled and again Nebuchadnezzar reacted. This time he destroyed Jerusalem utterly (see below).

Let us go back to Jehoiachin because his story is not over yet. He survived the ordeal and spent the next decades in prison in Babylon. The Bible does not reveal if he was sent to an ordinary or a luxury priosn, worthy of a king, even a rebellious one. We may assume the latter, because Jehoiachin survived for 37 more years.

Then, according to 2 Kings 25:27–30, a miracle happened:

> In the thirty-seventh year of the exile of Jehoiachin king of Judah, in the year Awel-Marduk became king of Babylon, he released Jehoiachin king of Judah from prison. He spoke kindly to him and gave him a seat of honor higher than those of the other kings who were with him in Babylon. So Jehoiachin put aside his prison clothes and for the rest of his life ate regularly at the king's table. Day by day the king gave Jehoiachin a regular allowance as long as he lived.

This sounds like a fairy tale, but there is some corroborating evidence for the story in ancient Babylonian chronicles pertaining to the reigns of king Nebuchadnezzar II and his son Awel-Marduk.

Neo-Babylonian records on Jehoiachin

The deeds of the might king Nebuchadnezzar II and the other Neo-Babylonian kings are recorded in a series of clay tablets found in the 19th century that are now in the British Museum. They are aptly called the Babylonian Chronicles (Fig. 8.2). Most are unprovenanced, that is, no exact findspot is known and they were bought by the museum from antiquities dealers.

For our purpose the most interesting is the so-called Jerusalem Chronicle, detailing the events discussed above. It says:

> In the seventh year [of Nebuchadnezzar] in the month Chislev [Nov/Dec] the king of Babylon assembled his army, and after he had invaded the land of Hatti [Syria/Palestine] he laid siege to the city of Judah. On the second day of the month of Adar

Figure 8.2 Clay tablet with the Jerusalem Chronicle (© Trustees of the British Museum Creative Commons Licence CC BY-SA 4.0).

[16 March] he conquered the city and took the king [Jehoiachin] prisoner. He installed in his place a king [Zedekiah] of his own choice, and after he had received rich tribute, he sent forth to Babylon.

The release from prison is not documented in the available chronicles. Not all have survived but even if we had all the chronicles that were ever written one cannot expect a triviality such as the release of an old man as from prison to be recorded.

That said, other clay tablets do contain information about the former king of Judah. When excavating in the city of Babylon (1899–1914) Robert Koldewey found almost 300 clay tablets that documented the rations given out by the royal storehouses. Many make reference to the years of king Nebuchadnezzar's reign and so we know they are dating to the 10th–35th years of his reign, that is between 594 and 569 BC. The tablets are now in the Pergamon Museum of Berlin (Fig. 8.3).

Surprisingly, four tablets of lists mention Jehoiachin who is called respectively Ia-'-u-kin, Ia-'-kin, Ia-ku-ú-ki-nu or the king of Ia-a-hu-du (Judah) or Ia-a-ku-du. Here two of these variants are given.

> 10 sila of oil to ... [Ia]-'-kin, king of Ia-[a-hu-du]
> 2½ sila of oil to the [five so]ns of the king of Ia-a-hu-du
> 4 sila to eight men from Ia-a-hu-da-a-a ...
>
> 1½ sila for three carpenters from Arvad, ½ sila each
> 11½ sila for eight ditto from Byblos, 1 sila each ...
> 3½ sila for seven ditto, ½ sila each
> ½ sila for Nabû-êtir the carpenter
> 10 sila to Ia-ku-ú-ki-nu, the son of the king of Ia-ku-du
> 2½ sila for the five sons of the king of Ia-ku-du through Qana'a

These lists pertain to the period that Jehoiachin was supposedly a prisoner during Nebuchadnezzar's reign not from the period after he was released from prison and 'received a regular allowance as long as he lived', according to the biblical texts. He was not the only one receiving food from the royal storehouses. His sons

Figure 8.3 Clay tablet mentioning king Jehoiachin (Pergamon Museum, Berlin Creative Commons Licence CC0 1.0 Universal).

and other men from Judah are mentioned, as well as carpenters from Byblos, Arvad, Tyre and Lyddia. They all are apportioned grain (or bread) and olive oil, and possibly other goods such as wine, beer and clothing. However, the only product mentioned by name in these lists is olive oil.

It is clear from the lists that Jehoiachin receives much more oil than the others. While the carpenters from Arvad get a half sila of olive oil each (about half a litre); those from Byblos get 1 sila each; the five sons of the king 2.5 sila together; the king of Judah gets 10 sila. Perhaps he had to feed his personal household from this amount?

According to some scholars this means that he must have had a certain amount of freedom and was not lingering in a dark prison. One may assume that the carpenters mentioned were put to good use and were working for the king; the rations mentioned then were their salary.

Jehoiachin, who is respectfully named king of Judah every time he is mentioned, even though he was not a king anymore, was probably not working but treated as a guest and allowed to have his own small retinue. He was, so to speak, eating at the kings table, even if only metaphorically.

Why then does the Bible depict him in prison all the long years of Nebuchadnezzar's reign, only to be rescued by his successor? Is it because the biblical writers were loath to say anything positive of this Babylonian king who, after all, had destroyed Jerusalem and the temple in 587 BC? Better then to ascribe the good treatment of the former king of Judah to his heir Awel-Marduk.

More exiles

In 597 BC the elite of Jerusalem was sent into exile by the Neo-Babylonians: commanders of the army, officials of the king, and the whole royal court, 'the entire force of seven thousand fighting men, strong and fit for war, and a thousand skilled workers and artisans.' (2 Kings 24:16). Those that remained are called 'the poorest people of the land' (2 Kings 24:14). They were the ones not belonging to the elite – the farmers and day labourers, the cooks and cleaners, so to speak.

Judah was not utterly destroyed, nor was Jerusalem, and a new king was appointed by Nebuchadnezzar. One may assume that it was not in Babylonia's interest to crush

Judah's economy and the grain and olive oil it provided for the king's army. When, however, the newly appointed king Zedekiah revolted again, it meant the end of the Judean kingdom, even as a vassal state.

The biblical texts tell a chilling story in Jeremiah 52.

> Now Zedekiah rebelled against the king of Babylon. So in the ninth year of Zedekiah's reign, on the tenth day of the tenth month, Nebuchadnezzar king of Babylon marched against Jerusalem with his whole army. They encamped outside the city and built siege works all around it. The city was kept under siege until the eleventh year of King Zedekiah. By the ninth day of the fourth month the famine in the city had become so severe that there was no food for the people to eat. Then the city wall was broken through, and the whole army fled.

King Zedekiah was blinded but not before he had to watch his sons being killed. The city was burnt to the ground, including the temple, the royal palace and most of the houses. The remainder of the population was sent into exile. The Babylonians 'left behind the rest of the poorest people of the land to work the vineyards and fields' (Jer. 52:16). This all happened in 587 BC. In Jer. 52: 27–30 the number of people sent to Babylonia is mentioned:

> So Judah went into captivity, away from her land. This is the number of the people Nebuchadnezzar carried into exile: in the seventh year, 3,023 Jews; in Nebuchadnezzar's eighteenth year, 832 people from Jerusalem; in his twenty-third year, 745 Jews taken into exile by Nebuzaradan the commander of the imperial guard. There were 4,600 people in all.

One might be surprised by the small number of people sent away but remember that many inhabitants had already been exiled in 597 BC. It seems that the exiles were not sent all at the same time, but in groups, with sometimes many years in between. Whenever the Babylonians needed people to till the land or to work on their large building projects, inhabitants from the subjugated regions were sent there.

Babylonian inscriptions from the year that Nebuchadnezzar destroyed Jerusalem have not been unearthed, so we do not have the king's own words for it. However, archaeology confirms this sorry state of affairs. In every excavation in the city remains from the destruction of 587 BC have been uncovered: torn-down city walls, burnt houses and rooms filled with stones and debris from the collapsed walls, packed full with broken household pottery, loom-weights, stone vessels, remains of meals, and metal objects. Iron and bronze arrowheads provide evidence of the fighting that occurred. Jerusalem was utterly destroyed and would remain so for decades.

Judah as a Babylonian province

After Nebuchadnezzar's final campaign Judah became a province of the Babylonian empire, with a governor who settled in Mitzpah (2 Kings 25:22). Strangely enough the Bible is largely silent on the situation of this Babylonian province and of the people that stayed behind. Babylonian sources do not deal specifically with Judah either.

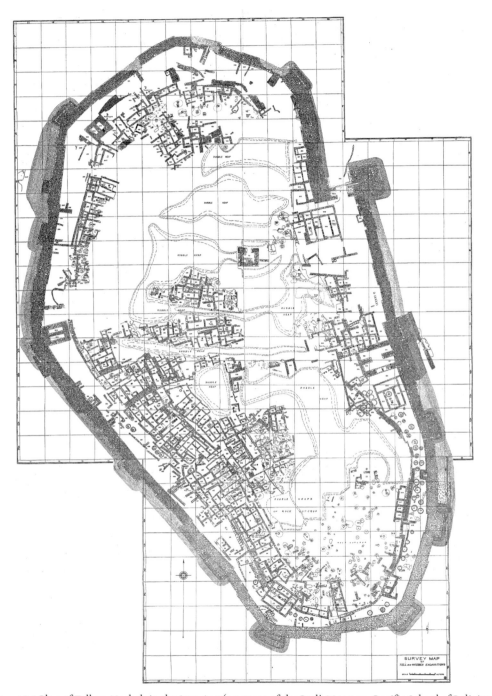

Figure 8.4 Plan of Tell en-Nasbeh in the Iron Age (courtesy of the Badè Museum, Pacific School of Religion).

בית

Al-Yahudu אֱל-יְהוּדוּ

Figure 8.5 One of the Al-Yahuda tablets (Creative Commons Licence CC BY-SA 4.0).

Mitzpah has been identified with Tell en-Nasbeh, a small town north-west of Jerusalem. The site was excavated between 1926 and 1935 and uncovered remains from several periods. The main period of occupation consisted of a fortified village or small town, dating to Iron Age II (*c.* 900–600 BC) (stratum 3), while stratum 2 comprised several four-room buildings of the Neo-Babylonian and Early Persian periods, built on top of the destroyed stratum 3 houses (Fig. 8.4). The Neo-Babylonian buildings were larger and more luxurious than the earlier ones, as would fit the residency of a governor.

Within a year of his appointment the first governor, Gedaliah, together with his staff and several Babylonian officials, was murdered by adversaries who were against the Babylonian occupation (2 Kings 25:25). After that the Bible is silent on the appointment of any new governor in Judah or the fate of Mizpah.

Yehuda texts

We know more of the fate of the exiles living in Babylonia who were settled in the regions around the capital Babylon and around Nippur in small towns or previously deserted villages. They were forced to work in agriculture and irrigation works to feed the many mouths of the ever growing Neo-Babylonian empire. They may also have worked on the grand building projects of the kings (see below).

Recently a series of clay tablets has been published that deal with the exiles from Judah (Fig. 8.5). The tablets were found in present-day Iraq near Birs Nimrud (ancient Borsippa), some 100 km south-west of Bagdad. There a village called al-Yahudu was inhabited by exiles. Al-Yahudu means 'the village of Judah' or 'the village of the Judaeans'. Yahudu may also be a reference to Jerusalem, which in Nebuchadnezzar's inscription mentioned above was simply called 'the city of Judah'.

These documents, written by a Babylonian scribe in the Akkadian language and in cuneiform script, were recorded between 572 and 484 BC, in the Neo-Babylonian and Early Persian periods. They are administrative texts such as marital arrangements, contracts for the sale and rent of livestock, testaments, house rentals, receipts for

Figure 8.6 Tower of Babel by Pieter Brueghel the Elder, 1563 (Museum Boijmans Van Beuningen, public domain).

the payment of dates and barley, documents pertaining to the acquirement of land in exchange for military services, and slavery transactions.

According to some scholars, the tablets show that the inhabitants of al-Yahudu were semi-independent and able to close agreements and buy and sell products, although they were also obliged to serve in the army and work on state projects. Others see this differently and interpret al-Yahudu not as an independent village but as a state farm. The farmers were each allotted a piece of land, meant to feed themselves as well as providing tribute for the state in the form of grain, dates, beer, cattle and silver. They were not free to move from their lands.

However this may be, after the exiles had received permission to return to the land of Israel by the Persian king Cyrus (see Chapter 2), many remained in Babylonia. Throughout the centuries that followed the Jewish community in Babylonia became an important part of the Jewish people and produced the Babylonian Talmud or Talmud Bavli in the 3rd–5th centuries AD.

The tower of Babylon

The sojourn in Babylonia of the elite of Judah, particularly the royal house, the priests and scribes, must have made a deep impact on these quite provincial people. Here they came in direct contact with the Mesopotamian culture and its grand myths and epic stories, some of which found their way into the Bible.

One of the most famous stories in the Bible is that of the Tower of Babel in Genesis 11:1–9 (Fig. 8.6). It said:

> Now the whole world had one language and a common speech.' When the people moved eastwards towards Babylonia, 'they said to each other, Come, let's make bricks and bake them thoroughly. They used brick instead of stone, and tar for mortar. Then they said, Come, let us build ourselves a city, with a tower that reaches to the heavens, so that we may make a name for ourselves; otherwise we will be scattered over the face of the whole earth.

The rest is 'history'. God became angry at this act of *hubris,* and confused their language and scattered them all over the earth. This story of people of one language building a tower and thereby angering the gods, is also known from an ancient Sumerian epic *Enmerkar and the Lord of Aratta.* This tower was no doubt a ziggurat, a large tower with a temple on top of it. The first temple towers can be ascribed to the Sumerians in the 4th millennium BC. From then on the towers grew steadily bigger and higher.

The tower in question – the ziggurat of Babylon – was part of the great building projects of king Nebuchadnezzar II when he enlarged and beautified the city. He built a large complex with temples, gates, procession roads and tombs, as well as a ziggurat for the city god Marduk. The beautiful Ishtar gate with its green-blue glazed tiles, now in the Pergamon museum, was part of this complex. The ziggurat itself could not be excavated; its tiles and glazed bricks had mostly disappeared as they had been re-used for other buildings. What remained was a large pile of rubble surrounded by water.

It is a lucky coincidence that we have written information on the ziggurat (Figs 8.7 and 8.8). One text from the time of king Nebuchadnezzar II gives a description of the tower in the king's own words: 'The tower, the eternal house, which I founded and built. I have completed its magnificence with silver, gold, other metals, stone, enamelled bricks, fir and pine.' Another inscription states: 'Etemenanki Zikkurat Babibli [Ziggurat of Babylon] I made it, the

Figure 8.7 Inscription of Nebuchadnezzar II commemorating the reconstruction of Etemenanki, the ziggurat at Babylon (Metropolitan Museum New York, Creative Commons Licence CC0 1.0 Universal).

Figure 8.8 Stone stele depicting king Nebukadnezzar II in front of Etemenanki. The king holds a papyrus in his hand with the plan of the (re)building of the temple. Above the tower is a plan of the temple. The original stele is quite damaged and white lines are inserted in the picture for easy reference (public domain).

wonder of the people of the world, I raised its top to heaven, made doors for the gates, and I covered it with bitumen and bricks.'

We have another eye witness: the Greek historian Herodotus visited Babylon in the 5th century BC, when Etemenanki was still standing. He wrote this about the temple complex:

> In the middle of the precinct there was a tower of solid masonry, a furlong [201 m] in length and breadth, upon which was raised a second tower, and on that a third, and so on up to eight. The ascent to the top is on the outside, by a path which winds round all the towers. When one is about half-way up, one finds a resting-place and seats, where persons can sit for some time on their way to the summit. On the topmost tower there is a spacious temple, and inside the temple stands a couch of unusual size, richly adorned, with a golden table by its side. There is no statue of any kind set up in the place, nor is the chamber occupied of nights by anyone but a single native woman, who, as the Chaldeans, the priests of this god, affirm, is chosen for himself by the deity out of all the women of the land.

How did an ancient Mesopotamian story on human *hubris* linked with the building of the ziggurat of Babylon end up in the Bible? One may assume that this happened in the time that the people of Judah were in close contact with the Babylonian architecture, and that would be in the period of the Exile. It is even possible that Judean exiles were forced to work on king Nebuchadnezzar's building projects. They must have been very impressed of the immense dimension of the tower and may have seen it as an attempt of the king to challenge the gods. Did he not say himself in a text: 'Etemenanki ... I made it, the wonder of the people of the world, I raised its top to heaven.'

Exile and return

The destruction of Jerusalem and the Exile to Babylonia were important moments in the history of the people of Israel. Most scholars believe that many biblical texts were produced then, when the Land was destroyed, its people dispersed and the situation seemed hopeless. Writing up the ancient stories, hymns and prayers provided support for the people in exile and became a blueprint after many exiles returned to the Land (see Chapter 2). Israel's identity was formed in these years. And it all began with a king, just 18 years old, making the wrong decision and paying a heavy price for that.

Texts from the Judean exiles have been unearthed in Babylon and provide insight in the lives they led in the villages were they were settled. It seems they were not badly off although some scholars warn us not to paint too rosy a picture of their situation.

It is remarkable that we have more information on the lives of the exiles than of the people who stayed behind. It is not even clear if Jerusalem was still inhabited and how the governor's residency Mizpah fared after the governor had been killed. Archaeological excavations pertaining to this period provide only sketchy and contradictory images.

The situation changed after king Cyrus of Persia defeated the Babylonian empire. Many exiles, not just Judeans, were allowed to return home with their possessions and the temple inventories that had been taken to Babylonia many years before. Many Judeans returned, many did not. Judah became a Persian province, where the returnees tried to build up a new community based on their holy books written during the Exile. The Bible books of Ezra and Nehemiah deal with this difficult period. Archaeology can contribute to this story, but the results are often difficult to interpret. More research is needed before we can paint a reliable picture of Judah and Israel in the Neo-Babylonian and Persian periods.

Chapter 9

In search of ... the prophet Balaam

Excavations in the Levant have unearthed many texts that throw light on the religions of its inhabitants; some inscriptions have already been encountered in these pages. There is one text that stands out. A prophet known from the Bible, Balaam, son of Beor, describes a vision he had whilst asleep (Fig. 9.1). When he wakes up, he gathers the people of the village around him and, overcome by emotion, he begins his narrative. After it had been excavated and published, the text received a considerable attention in journals and in the media and on the internet because it concerns a biblical figure. However, this text does not support the biblical story in any way –which is exactly what makes it so interesting.

The discovery of the text

March 17, 1967: on Tell Deir Alla in Jordan, an excavation team directed by Professor Henk Franken of Leiden University is in the final stages of the digging season (Fig. 9.2). Suddenly the foreman, Abu Said, who received his training from Kathleen Kenyon in Jericho, notices a small fragment of white wall plaster on the spoilheap and picks it up. When he turns it over, he sees what looks like some characters on the other side. He runs to the excavation camp and shows the seemingly innocent fragment to Franken. Franken immediately stops the work on the tell and goes in search of the place from where the fragment originated. There, it turns out, many more fragments with writing on them are lying on the ground.

The circumstances make it imperative to work with the utmost care. The inscription is written with plain ink on white lime plaster and fades rapidly when exposed to direct sunlight, so a Bedouin tent is placed over the find spot (Fig. 9.3). For the same reason a regular camera with flashlight cannot be used to document the fragile fragments. Quickly, an infrared camera is ordered from the Netherlands and flown in – there are no infrared cameras in Jordan at the time. The position of each plaster fragment in relation to those around it, as found, is maintained as much as possible and the combined fragments reinforced with plaster of Paris (Fig. 9.4).[1]

Bileam, op den Ezel : Numer: XXII.

Figure 9.1 Etching of the prophet Balaam with his donkey, made by Caspar Luyken in 1708 (Rijksmuseum Amsterdam, public domain).

Figure 9.2 Aerial photograph of Tell Deir Alla in 1962 (archive H. J. Franken).

Figure 9.3 Tell Deir Alla, tent set up while excavating the plaster text (archive H. J. Franken).

Figure 9.4 Tell Deir Alla, fragments of the Balaam text set in plaster (archive H. J. Franken).

The original findspot of the text is a small room, part of a larger complex (Fig. 9.5). The text was written on one of the walls and when the building collapsed in an earthquake, part of the wall fell with the text face down on the floor (combination II), while another part of the wall fell in the opposite direction, into the adjoining room (combination I).

Fitting the more than 100 fragments together turned out to be a major undertaking but, in the end, a large part of the text could be reconstructed. Together the two combinations (I and II) form an incomplete but coherent narrative. There remain many other fragments with parts of sentences and words that do not fit. The text itself is written with black ink, framed with red lines; some words are written in red ink. There also is a depiction of a sphinx. My favourite fragment comes right at the beginning of the inscription, where the writer apparently forgot to write a word and had to put it above the text (Fig. 9.6).

According to professor Hoftijzer, who published the text, it was written in what can best be described as a local dialect of Aramaic, the language spoken in the Aramaic polities to the north of Deir Alla. However, Deir Alla itself is situated in Gilead, a region that was at the time controlled by the kingdom of Israel, according to the Bible, and where Hebrew is assumed to have been the common language. For this reason some scholars maintain that the language of the inscription must be ancient Hebrew, Canaanite, or Ammonite. Another solution for this 'problem' is to assume that Gilead was not part of ancient Israel in that period but of Aram. Or maybe it was part of Israel politically, but the inhabitants spoke their own dialect ... On the basis of the shape of the alphabetic characters the text was dated to around 800 BC, a date confirmed by pottery later found in layers of the same phase.

The building in which the text was found stood in a small village. This village (phase IX of the excavated sequence) was further explored after 1972. In total about 15 houses have been excavated (see Fig. 9.5) but there must have been more because only part of the tell has been excavated. It was a prosperous settlement, situated on the crossroads of trade routes. Grinding stones were imported from north Jordan or south Syria while textiles woven in the village were sold on the local markets. The farmers cultivated wheat and barley, peas and bitter vetch, as well as lentils, flax, figs, grapes and pomegranates. They also had cattle, sheep and goats.

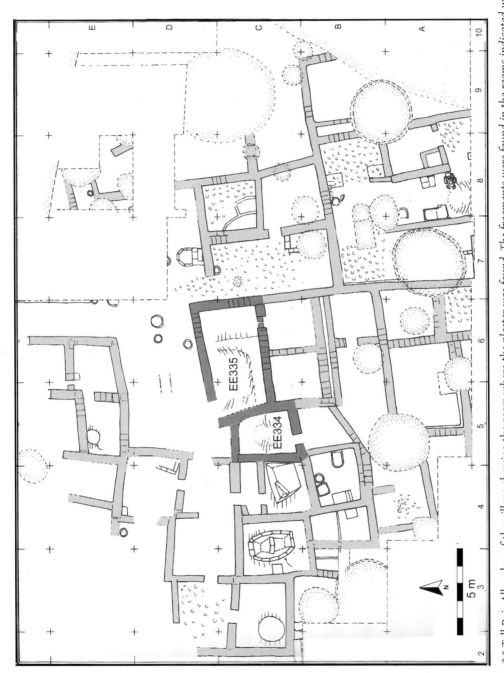

Figure 9.5 Tell Deir Alla, plan of the village showing the room where the plaster was found. The fragments were found in the rooms indicated with black lines (drawing E. van der Steen, © Margreet Steiner).

Figure 9.6 The Balaam inscription: the author forgot a word and wrote it above the text (courtesy Deir Alla Project).

The nature of the building itself has been widely debated. Was it a sanctuary? A school for scribes? It has even been suggested (by serious scholars) that it was a meeting place for local prophets – a suggestion that conjures up joyful images of local prophets sharing a quiet drink at the bar. Henk Franken, who excavated the site, suggests that the building functioned as an artificial 'cave', a place where people could spend the night in the presence of the text and thus receive visions and dreams. What made Deir Alla so special that it merited such a sanctuary we will never know.

Balaam, son of Beor, tells his story

The text as found consists of two major 'combinations'. Combination I tells the story of Balaam's dream (Fig. 9.7). The goddess Shagar is going to punish the people for something they have done and asks the 'congregation of the Shadday-gods' headed by the god El, for permission to do so. The gods agree with certain punishments: Shagar is allowed to 'break the bolts of heaven' (visit storm and thunder upon earth), as long as it does not last too long. She can disrupt the world order: the swift will mock the eagle, the deaf will hear from afar, a poor woman will mix herself a precious ointment of myrrh, a pupil will mock the wise. There will be droughts: where now the sheep graze, hares shall eat the grass. The order of everything will be turned upside down, and the result is chaos.

Combination II consists of less coherent fragments and is comprised mainly of curses. 'You will lie on your death bed ...' and 'no one will counsel you when you need counselling'. There is talk of 'a house in which no traveller shall enter' and of death snatching away a newborn babe.

Here follows the translation of Combination I, as published by Hoftijzer and Van der Kooij in 1976.

> The misfortunes of the Book of Balaam, son of Beor. A divine seer was he.
> The gods came to him at night.
> And he beheld a vision in accordance with El's utterance.
> They said to Balaam, son of Beor:
> So will it be done, with naught surviving.
> No one has seen [the likes of] what you have heard!

Figure 9.7 The Balaam inscription: drawing of Combination 1 (courtesy Deir Alla Project).

Balaam arose on the morrow;
He summoned the heads of the assembly to him,
And for two days he fasted, and wept bitterly.
Then his intimates entered into his presence,
and they said to Balaam, son of Beor,
Why do you fast, and why do you weep?
Then he said to them: Be seated, and I will relate to you what the Shaddai gods have planned,
And go, see the acts of the god!

The gods have banded together;
The Shaddai gods have established a council,
And they have said to [the goddess] Shagar:
Sew up, close up the heavens with dense cloud,
That darkness exist there, not brilliance;
Obscurity and not clarity;

So that you instill dread in dense darkness.
And – never utter a sound again!
It shall be that the swift and crane will shriek insult to the eagle,
And a nest of vultures shall cry out in response.
The stork, the young of the falcon and the owl,
The chicks of the heron, sparrow and cluster of eagles;
Pigeons and birds, [and fowl in the s]ky.
And a rod [shall flay the cat]tle;
Where there are ewes, a staff shall be brought.
Hares – eat together!
....
They heard incantations from afar
...
Then disease was unleashed
And all beheld acts of distress.
Shagar-and-Ashtar did not ...
The piglet [drove out] the leopard

There is an interesting combination of gods in this story: El, Shagar, the Shadday gods and Ashtar. El as encountered in Chapter 2 as the supreme deity of the Canaanite pantheon. Ashtar is a male deity who also figures in the Mesha Stele (Chapter 7). He is probably the male counterpart of the female Ashtarte.

Shagar is an goddess not known in the Canaanite or Phoenician pantheon. The Bible mentions 'the shagar of thy cattle and the ashtarot of thy sheep (Deuteronomy 7:13, 28:4, 18, 51). This is usually translated as 'the fruit of thy cattle and the flocks of thy sheep'. With this translation, of shagar as 'fruit' and ashtarot as 'flocks', the translators do not do justice to the original text. Apparently, Shagar and Ashtarte were goddesses guarding the fertility of the flocks and were well-known in ancient Israel.

The Shadday-gods are not mentioned in the Canaanite pantheon. They seem to represent a particular group of gods. In the Bible El Shadday is one of the names of the god of Israel. This is usually translated as God the Almighty, the All-powerful. The precise meaning of the word *shadday* is being debated. It is often assumed to mean 'from the mountains'.

Balaam and the Bible

The Bible has a lot to say about Balaam, son of Beor. The story runs from Numbers 21–24. It is a somewhat confusing story, involving Balaam himself, and king Balak of Moab and his servants, but also an angel and, of course, Balaam's donkey.

The story is part of the narrative on the journey that brought the people of Israel from Egypt to the Holy Land: the Exodus. On their way north they want to pass through the kingdom of Moab. But Balak, the king of Moab, does not want to let them in and invokes the aid of the famous prophet Balaam, who must curse them.

At first, Balaam refuses because the God of Israel forbids him to, but then God relents and allows Balaam to go. Then, when Balaam sets out, his way is blocked by an angel, up to three times. You may be familiar with the famous story of the donkey that perceives the angel (while Balaam does not) and refuses to go on. Balaam curses his donkey and hits her with his stick to make her move but then the donkey begins to speak: 'What have I done to you, that you have hit me three times?' Then, at last, Balaam also sees the angel. He gives in and makes a move to return home. Then the angel tells him to go to Moab after all. In the end Balaam arrives at the king's palace and tries to curse the Israelites three times but every time a blessing comes out of his mouth instead.

A direct link between the biblical text and the inscription is difficult to establish. If the Exodus stories do have a historical core (which is far from certain), the entry into the Promised Land must be dated to around 1200 BC – which is much earlier than the Balaam inscription as found.

There are also major differences in content between the biblical narrative and the text of the inscription. The inscription has a clear Canaanite context. The ancient Canaanite gods play a major part, as does the goddess Shagar, while Israel's god is not mentioned at all. The text of the inscription is Aramaic, not Hebrew. In the Bible, on the other hand, Balaam is a follower of YHWH, who uses him to bless the people of Israel. The two stories do, however, also have certain things in common. Balaam is a prophet who, in both stories, has direct access to the world of the gods and who talks to them, either in dreams or in visions. He is a famous exorcist and pronouncer of curses. In the Bible the king of Moab charters him to curse the people of Israel – his special field of expertise. In the Deir Alla texts he also curses to his heart's content.

Who was Balaam?

After the find of the inscription of Deir Alla, how should we see Balaam? Does the inscription prove that he really existed? Did he live in the region of Deir Alla as some scholars suggest? Was he a famous prophet in the region? Why is it that this long inscription was written on the wall of a building in a small village and not in the temple of an important city? It is unlikely that the villagers were literate so could they have been able to read it at all? In other words, why was that particular inscription written on that particular wall, what was its *Sitz im Leben*?

To start with the last question: nobody knows. This is a unique find, and unique finds are hard to interpret. The majority of long inscriptions that figure in this book, such as the Tel Dan inscription and the Mesha Stele, were written to glorify the deeds of kings or they are inscriptions on statues in temples. The Balaam inscription is completely different. One can imagine that a small sanctuary existed at Deir Alla, with a priest(ess) who would, on occasion, recite the text for the local population or for visiting pilgrims. This sanctuary may have been dedicated to a local deity, possibly the goddess Shagar, who plays the leading part in the text. Did a prophet named Balaam live in Deir Alla? That is a nice thought, of course, but unfortunately, the fact that somebody has written a text about him does not mean that he actually lived there – or that he existed at all.

What, then, is the relation between the inscription and the biblical narrative? There are similarities, but there are also major differences. The inscription was written down around 800 BC but that does not have to be the date of the origin of this story. It may well have been part of an older oral tradition circulating in the region. So, the inscription does not tell us when the story was invented, nor whether Balaam was a real person.

As said previously, if the Exodus stories have a historical core the entry of the Israelites can be dated to around 1200 BC – much earlier than the inscription. However, these biblical stories have been written down much later, and it is quite possible that the editors of the Bible were familiar with story cycles and traditions about a prophet named Balaam, and that they used him in one of their own narratives. What we can deduce from these two texts is that in Gilead, and possibly also outside Gilead, a collection of stories was passed on about a prophet who was a son of Beor, who had access to the world of the gods and from them received dreams and visions, and who was an expert in cursing. Eventually those stories ended up on the wall of a village sanctuary in Jordan, and in the pages of the Bible.

Note

1 More on the discovery of this text in Steiner and Wagemakers 2019.

Chapter 10

In search of ... the goddess Asherah

Reading the Bible in the 'traditional' way, it is easy to conclude that Israel's god was male and had no female consort or partner, in contrast to most other deities in the regions around Israel. However, if you read the Bible with an open mind you will find many traces of other religious practices such as the veneration of female deities like Asherah and the 'Queen of Heaven' (Fig. 10.1). This deviant picture of Israel's religion seems to be confirmed by archaeological finds.

In this chapter the possibility of there being a consort of YHWH will be researched. First possible traces of a goddess in the Bible will be considered, then we will look at several archaeological discoveries and finally the conclusions will be discussed that can be drawn from these sources.

Traces of female deities in the Bible

The famous book by Raphael Patai, *The Hebrew Goddess*, was my first encounter with the idea that not only male gods were worshipped in the Bible – the god of Israel YHWH and the 'idols' Baal and Moloch – but that traces can be found of the veneration of one or more goddesses as well. Patai wrote his book in 1967 and since then it has been reprinted and re-edited numerous times. Patai searched for the feminine element in the Bible and discussed, among others, the occurance of the goddesses Asherah, Astarte and Anat, the cherubim, and the *shekhinah* (wisdom). Also, in later Jewish traditions such as the Kabbalah, he encounters the feminine in the form of Matronit and Lilith.

Later books written from a feminist perspective, such as Merlin Stone's *When God was a Woman* (1978), confirmed and expanded on his ideas. A recent contribution to this discussion is William Dever's *Did God have a Wife?* (2005). This book caused quite a stir, particularly because Dever rather simplified aspects of the discussion – the title says it all! It turns out that Israel's religion was less monotheistic and less masculine than I had been taught. So here is a short discussion of three goddesses that figure in the Bible; Asherah, Astarte and the 'Queen of Heaven'.

Asherah

The name Asherah appears some 40 times in the Hebrew Bible. Translations of the Bible, however, do not always make this clear. In the King James Version (KJV) of 1611 the name is not mentioned at all because it is consistently translated as 'a grove' for idol worship (Deuteronomy 7:5) or as an 'idol in a grove' (1 Kings 15:13). In the modern New King James Version (NKJV) the name appears only six times, as an indignant 'obscene image of Asherah' (1 Kings 15:13; 2 Chronicles 15:16) or a 'carved image of Asherah' (2 Kings 21:7).

In the Bible, Asherah is often depicted as the consort of the Phoenician god Baal (Judges 3:7). However, in the Canaanite pantheon of the Late Bronze Age she is the consort of the supreme deity El, the mother of all the gods, and definitely not the consort of Baal

Figure 10.1 Limestone stele featuring the goddess Qetesh or Qadesh standing on a lion, posed between the Egyptian god Min and the Canaanite god Resheph. Qetesh was adopted in Egypt from the Canaanite pantheon during the Bronze Age. She is often equated with Asherah (Louvre Museum Creative Commons Licence CC BY-SA 2.0 fr).

(see Chapter 2). In the Bible she is regularly associated with her symbol, a tree or a wooden pole (or 'a sacred pillar' in the NKJV). Such a pole was sometimes erected in the temple in Jerusalem, according to 2 Kings 21:7:

> He even set a carved image of Asherah that he had made, in the house of which the Lord had said to David and to Solomon his son, 'In this house and in Jerusalem, which I have chosen out of all the tribes of Israel, I will put My name forever.'

In 2 Kings 23:6–7 the name Asherah is translated as a 'wooden image' in the NKJV and as a 'grove' in the KJV. These verses also refer to women (servants of the cult?) weaving garments for Asherah in the temple quarters.

Because Asherah is mentioned so many times in the Bible (though in translations not always by her name) you might expect that she was widely venerated in Ancient Israel. But there are reasons not to jump to this conclusion too hastily. In Israel personal names were often theophoric, which means that they contained the (sometimes partial) name of a deity. YHWH, Baal, Shams and even Bes appear in personal names, but never the goddess Asherah.[2] Marjo Korpel, who wrote an article on Asherah, sees this as an indication that the veneration of Asherah in Israel was not as widespread as that of her consort Baal.

Astarte

In the Canaanite pantheon Astarte or Ashtoret was the consort of Baal and a lesser deity of hunting. For the later Phoenicians she became an important goddess. In the

Bible I encountered her only as 'Ashtoret the abomination of the Sidonians' (NKJV) or 'Ashtoreth the vile goddess of the Sidonians' (New International Version). Sidon was long the major harbour city of the Phoenicians and, as a result, Phoenicians were generally called Sidonians in the Bible. So she is never seen as an Israelite goddess. The only exception is the mention of 'the shagar of thy cattle and the ashtarot of thy sheep (Deuteronomy 7:13, 28:4, 18, 51; see Chapter 9). In Hellenistic and Roman times Astarte became the most important goddess in the Levant and temples dedicated to her were erected everywhere. She eventually became associated with the northern Levantine goddess Atargatis and with Egyptian Isis.

The Queen of Heaven

In the biblical book of Jeremiah, which focuses on the destruction of Jerusalem by the Babylonians in 587 BC, we find several references to the veneration of a goddess who bears the epithet 'Queen of Heaven'. In Jeremiah 7 the prophet is ordered by God to go and preach at the gate that leads to the temple of Jerusalem. Here he rebukes the people for their corrupt practices. In Jeremiah 7:17–18 God points one of these practices out to Jeremiah:

> Do you not see what they are doing in the towns of Judah and in the streets of Jerusalem? The children gather wood, the fathers light the fire, and the women knead the dough and make cakes to offer to the Queen of Heaven. They pour out drink offerings to other gods to arouse my anger.

In Egypt, where some of the inhabitants of Jerusalem had fled after its destruction by Nebuchadnezzar in 587 BC, the Queen of Heaven was also venerated by them. Even worse, when Jeremiah preached to the exiles there, his audience was convinced that their present misery was punishment for stopping to venerate her – at the insistence of Jeremiah. They tell him:

> We will not listen to the message you have spoken to us in the name of the *Lord*! We will certainly do everything we said we would: We will burn incense to the Queen of Heaven and will pour out drink offerings to her just as we and our ancestors, our kings and our officials did in the towns of Judah and in the streets of Jerusalem. At that time we had plenty of food and were well off and suffered no harm. But ever since we stopped burning incense to the Queen of Heaven and pouring out drink offerings to her, we have had nothing and have been perishing by sword and famine. The women added, When we burned incense to the Queen of Heaven and poured out drink offerings to her, did not our husbands know that we were making cakes impressed with her image and pouring out drink offerings to her? (Jeremiah 44:16–19)

This text suggests that the Queen of Heaven had enjoyed a long veneration in Judah, not only by the common people, but also among the elite: '... as we and our ancestors, our kings and our officials did in the towns of Judah and in the streets of Jerusalem.'

A whole body of literature has been generated on the question of which deity is meant by the Queen of Heaven. One suggestion is the Mesopotamian goddess Ishtar, who was also known as the Queen of Heaven. Mesopotamian deities were not unknown in Judah. The god Tammuz, consort of Ishtar, may also have been venerated in the temple in Jerusalem. He was a deity of fertility, who (in Assyria) died each autumn when the grain had been milled; a festival was then held to lament his death. Ezekiel 8:14 states: 'Then he brought me to the entrance of the north gate of the house of the Lord, and I saw women sitting there, mourning the god Tammuz'. This may refer to said festival, which seems to have been celebrated in the temple. Another reference to Mesopotamian gods may be found in 2 Kings 23:11 where mention is made of 'horses and chariots that kings of Judah had dedicated to the sun'. These objects had been set in one of the courtyards of the temple. They may have been connected with the Assyrian sun god Sin, who was carried across the sky in his horse-drawn chariot.

Other possibilities that are mentioned to identify the Queen of Heaven are the Canaanite/Phoenician goddesses Astarte, Anat and Asherah, or the Egyptian goddess Isis. The verses in Jeremiah do not give enough clues to decide upon a specific identity. Perhaps she is an amalgamation of various goddesses venerated in the region.

Archaeological discoveries

Various inscriptions have been found which mention Asherah by name and figurines and incense altars discovered in excavations are often associated with this deity.

Kuntillet Ajrud

In the 1970s a number of inscriptions were found that seem to indicate that a goddess was venerated as YHWH's consort in Israel. I am careful with my phrasing here because there are quite a number of pitfalls. The original discovery was made by Ze'ev Meshel at the site of Kuntillet Ajrud in the Sinai desert, where he was excavating a fortress that contained a sanctuary. The sanctuary consisted of a couple of rooms with benches along the walls. On the walls of the rooms were painted images and texts and he also found also a number of painted pottery jars. The site was located on a trade route that went through Sinai and is therefore interpreted as a fortified caravanserai or trading post. Radiocarbon dating places the building of the fortress around 800 BC. It seems to have been abandoned shortly after 745 BC.

The text on the sherds of two large vessels (pithoi A and B) in particular has drawn a lot of attention because the name of YHWH is mentioned together with the name Asherah (Fig. 10.2).

Here is a translation of some of the texts:

> I bless you by the YHWH of Teman and by his Asherah.
> May he bless you and keep you and be with my lord.

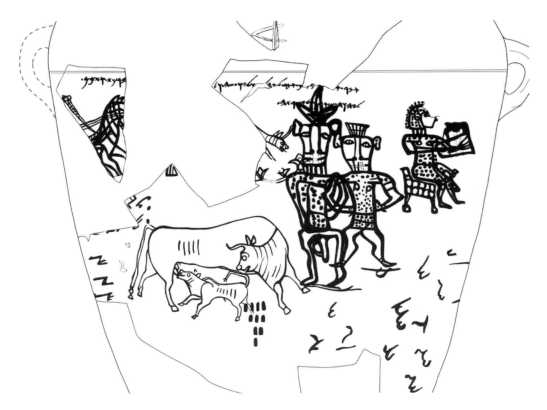

Figure 10.2 Drawing of a scene on a pithos sherd from Kuntillet Ajrud with the inscription 'Yahweh and his Asherah'. It is not clear what is depicted here. Are these the god of Israel and his consort, or just random figures doodled on a sherd? (public domain).

> I bless you by the YHWH of Teman and by his Asherah.
> Whatever he requests for a man may it be favoured.
> Let YHWH give him according to his hart desire.

> I bless you by YHWH of Samaria and by his Asherah.

These are apparently (copies of) letters with a greeting formula that seem to have been common in those days: 'I bless you by YHWH and his Asherah'. The record of various manifestations of YHWH (YHWH of Teman, YHWH of Samaria) mentioned together with 'his Asherah' has stirred some strong emotions – search for 'Kuntilled Ajrud' on the internet.

Meindert Dijkstra has pointed out that the inscriptions (and the rather clumsy drawings) are unlikely to have been written on the complete vessels. He sees the texts as ostraca: copies of letters on pot sherds; or even as the pottering of a bored clerk, doodling and practising standard formulas on potsherds to pass the time.

Figure 10.3 Inscription above and below the impression of a hand carved in a limestone pillar at Khirbet el-Qom (public domain).

That sounds a bit too contemporary for my taste although he is right to point out that these texts are not religious but rather polite standard formulas used in letters.

The fact that the phrase 'YHWH and his Asherah' was used as standard formulas in letters is shocking enough. Nowhere in the Bible is Asherah mentioned in connection with the God of Israel, nor are there any references to the YHWH of Teman, probably a district or town in Edom, or to the YHWH of Samaria, the capital of the northern kingdom of Israel (see Chapter 6). One may assume that a temple dedicated to YHWH (and his Asherah?) existed in those towns, but in Samaria no temple has been discovered.

The pottery found in the fortress of Kuntillet Ajrud was not locally made but consisted of vessels imported from Judah, Israel and Phoenicia. The majority came from Judah: the painted pithoi had all been manufactured in or near Jerusalem. There were also vessels from northern Israel and from Ashdod along the coast. These provenances support the interpretation of the site as a caravanserai. The traders travelling through the Negev used the site to rest for a while. They transported their wares to and from Israel, Judah and the coast, and visited the small shrine where they brought gifts for the gods they venerated, YHWH and Asherah foremost among them.

Khirbet el-Qom

Another inscription was found in Khirbet el-Qom, 14 km west of Hebron (Fig. 10.3). A stone, found in a grave that can be dated to the 8th century BC, reads:

> Uriyahu the honourable has written this
> Blessed is/be Uriyahu by Yahweh
> And [because?] from his oppressors by his asherah he has saved him
> [written] by Oniyahu
> ... by his asherah
> ... and his asherah

Again here the combination of YHWH and 'his' Asherah, and again the phrase seems to be used in the standard formula of a blessing.

Cult stands

Another source of information on a possible goddess venerated in Israel is presented by the many cult stands that have been excavated. Cult stand are large stands or small tables made of clay or stone. Some show remains of black soot on the top which suggests that they have been used to burn incense or other fragrant substances. Sometimes they served as a stand for a bowl containing fruits or other offerings or perhaps they were used as the base for the statue of a deity. Some of these are simple in shape and unadorned, while others are complicated affairs, richly decorated. An example of such a richly decorated cult stand was found in Tanaach (Fig. 10.4). It is 54 cm high, and has four registers, with elaborate decoration on the front and figures of lions and sphinxes on the sides.

Figure 10.4 Cult stand from Tanaach (public domain).

Its top register consists of a winged sun disc over an animal (a calf or a horse), flanked by pillars topped by spiral scrolls (volutes). The winged sun disc is the sun god's symbol. The next register shows the tree of life flanked on each side by a climbing goat and some lions (or lionesses) next to them. Below this are two sphinxes. The bottom register shows a naked woman holding on to two lionesses (Fig. 10.5). She is, without doubt, the goddess to whom the stand is dedicated. This goddess could well be Asherah, as this deity is often associated with lions and the tree of life, as we have also seen at Kuntillet Ajrud. However, her name is not mentioned on the object.

Figure 10.5 Detail of the Tanaach stand, showing a female figure, possibly Asherah, accompanied by two lions (courtesy Paul Butler).

Some cult stands are made in the shape of a building, sometimes with depictions of human figures, often a man and a woman, or of animals in the doorway. The majority have been found in Transjordan; a beautiful example from Ataruz is depicted in Figure 7.7. It is generally assumed that these models represent a sanctuary, with a god or a pair of gods in front of it – not inside, or we would not see them. Some remarkable examples have also been found in Rehov in the western Jordan Valley (Fig. 10.6). In an article entitled *To What God?*

Figure 10.6 Cult stand excavated at Tel Rehov with two figures standing in the door opening of a building (Oren Rozen (CC BY-SA 4.0)).

Altars and a House Shrine from Tel Rehov Puzzle Archaeologists, the excavators of that site have tried to identity the deities to which these altars were dedicated. They propose that 'the Canaanite population of Rehov retained its traditional religious practices, worshiping deities like Baal and Asherah. [...] The altars and house shrine from Tel Rehov were probably used in the local private cult practiced in homes and workshops; offerings were made for both personal well-being and industrial success.'

Figurines

Many figurines have been found, particularly in Judah. Figurines are miniature statuettes made of clay. Most depict women but there are also male figurines (often horse riders), various animals and even furniture. Small figurines have been found all over the Levant as well as in Greece and on Cyprus. Sometimes it is clear that they represent a deity, as in the case of the depictions of the Phoenician *dea nutrix*, the goddess of fertility (Fig. 10.7), or the Syrian gods Reshef or Baal (see Fig. 2.5). These statuettes can be identified as deities because of the 'divine' attributes they display: their hairstyle, a helmet, their dress or stance, a thunderbolt, or a shield. Sometimes they stand on a bull, or are flanked by two lions, while some female figures are supporting their breasts.

The Judean figurines have no such distinctive divine attributes, and so it is not certain that they represent deities. The women are pillar figurines, 10–20 cm in height (Fig. 10.8). The top half with the neck, arms and breasts is solid, the bottom half hollow and shapeless. The head is made separately in a mould and then attached to the body. Some figurines have a bird's head – a ball of clay that has been roughly pinched into shape. Horse riders are crudely made and badly finished, as are the animal figurines. Most of the time it is unclear whether we are looking at a cow, a sheep or a horse.

Many scholars assume that the female pillar figurines represent a goddess. Others have pointed out that any 'divine' attribute is missing, that the figurines have been crudely and quickly made, and that they are rarely found in a cultic context but usually in houses or burials. And here is something extraordinary: the figurines are usually described (by mostly male scholars) as 1) nude; 2) holding their breasts, just like the *dea nutrix*; and 3) in possession of large breasts, because of the focus on their life-giving and nurturing aspect and (of course) their sexuality. The German biblical scholar Robert Wenning speaks about 'den Aspekt des Entblössung und der erotischen Offerte durch Stutzen und präsentieren der nackten Brüsste.' (the aspect of nudity and of the erotic presentation, through supporting and presenting the naked breasts).

I have analysed a number of figurines from Jerusalem, and in contrast to the above, I found the following:

1) The women are not naked. When analysing some of the figurines under the microscope we found remains of red and white paint on their bodies as well as on their faces. The cheeks are painted red, the eyes outlined in black and the eyeballs are white while the pupils are black. Their bodies are painted in patterns of stripes or diamonds, no doubt representing a dress or robe. Vulva and navel are therefore not indicated, something about which a scholar in the 1960s expressed surprise – since, if the statuettes were naked (as he assumed) vulva and navel would have to be visible.

2) Most figurines do not hold or support their breasts. Unlike the *dea nutrix*, who holds her hands horizontally as a support (Fig. 10.7), these figurines mostly have their hands pressed flat against their chest or belly. This, I think, conveys a different meaning, namely the wish for a safe pregnancy.

Figure 10.7 Terracotta plaque from Gezer, showing the dea nutrix, the goddess of fertility (courtesy Paul Butler).

3) As far as the large breasts are concerned: first, it is not at all certain that in antiquity breasts had the same sexual connotation as they have today; they may rather have simply been associated with the feeding of babies. Secondly, one needs to be fairly prejudiced to define the breasts on these pillar figurines as very large. This interpretation probably derives from a figurine that was found in Jerusalem who does indeed have very large breasts. In fact, on all figurines the breasts are prominently shaped but not very large.

I have interpreted these figurines (in an article of 1997) as votive offerings to a deity, not necessarily YHWH or Asherah, symbolising something the supplicant wanted dearly – in this case pregnancy and many children. Similarly, animal figurines could represent the wish for lots of cattle, and horse-and-riders for the safe homecoming of a warrior.

Figure 10.8 Judean pillar figurine (Hanay, CC BY-SA 3.0).

Other scholars have interpreted these figurines differently. The female figurines would represent the goddess Asherah or perhaps they are toys, which would explain the general coarseness and the small size. Erin Darby, who has made the most extensive study to date, argues in her book *Interpreting Judean Pillar Figurines: Gender and Empire in Judean Apotropaic Ritual* (2014) that the figurines were in all probability associated with protection and healing in the household and may have been set up in doorways or room corners. She points out that they are never found in so-called cult corners of small shrines, let alone in temples, but always in domestic contexts. According to her the fact that they were made of humble, cheap and very breakable clay is a clear indication that they do not represent a major goddess.

However one wishes to interpret the figurines, it is doubtful that they are images of Asherah. But without a window into the thinking of the people who made and used these objects, they remain difficult to understand. Ziony Zevit, writing about the religion of Ancient Israel, states: 'They are all ceramic expressions in a language whose conventions we have barely recognized and which contemporary scholars do not yet understand.'

Did God have a wife?

So what can we conclude from the biblical text and the archaeological finds discussed in this chapter? Did God really have a wife? Or, to put it more generally: did YHWH have a female consort? In other words, was a female deity venerated in Ancient Israel, whether or not as part of the official cult?

There are enough indications to justify a positive answer. The clues in the Bible and in the texts found in Kuntillet Ajrud and Khirbet el-Qom do not seem to leave much room for doubt. But we have to tread careful here. As Marjo Korpel pointed out, there are no personal names with Asherah as a theophoric element in the Bible or in inscriptions, suggesting that the Asherah cult was not very widespread or important in Israel (see above). Other scholars have noted that Asherah is often depicted as or symbolised by a wooden pole, which could mean that, rather than a deity, she is (or had become in the Late Iron Age) a cultic object.

Andre Lemaire thinks that the grammatical construct 'his Asherah' as found in the inscriptions, is never used for a personal name in Hebrew and that therefore

Asherah cannot represent a person (deity), but is an object: he suggests a sacred tree or grove. Trees and groves were venerated in many places in Ancient Israel, much to the displeasure of the prophets. According to Lemaire these objects would have become increasingly personalised, as suggested by the Kuntillet Ajrud inscriptions, in which Asherah has almost become a consort. Other biblical scholars, such as Judith Hadley, suggest a movement in the opposite direction. In the more ancient texts Asherah would have been a deity, but in the later texts she became a cultic object. However this may be, we have traced the goddess, but to claim convincingly that we know how she was venerated in Ancient Israel – that is not (yet) possible.

Note

1 Theophoric names are, for example Daniel, which means 'my judge is El', or Joshua (Yehu-shua): 'YHWH is saviour'. Many place and personal names include not only the theophoric elements of YHWH or El, but surprisingly also of the Phoenician god Baal, the Philistine supreme deity Dagon, the sun god Shams and the Egyptian god Bes. One of the sons of Saul is called Eshbaal ('man of Baal'), while his other son is called Jonathan ('YHWH has given' – Jo being an abbreviation of YHWH). The name of the Israelite hero Samson includes the name Shams.

Chapter 11

In search of ... the temple of Jerusalem

This chapter searches not for a particular person, family clan or deity mentioned in the Bible, but for a building: the Jerusalem temple. One could fill a whole library room with literature investigating that elusive building. Why is it so hard to find? Did it actually exist? Did Solomon build it and, if he did, where was it located (Fig. 11.1)? Has anybody ever found traces of it? Or is the whole thing no more than a myth? And what about the temple built by king Herod? What do we know about that?

This chapter is investigating those questions and takes a look at other temples dedicated to the god of Israel, in ancient Israel and abroad, and at some forged inscriptions that were thought to be connected to the temple of Jerusalem.

Dwelling of the Gods

In the ancient Near East, the temple was the dwelling place of the gods. This was where the deity resided and his or her presence was often symbolised by the statue of the deity or a standing stone or stele. Therefore the Semitic word for temple is *bitu* or *beth*, meaning 'house'.

This also implies that the function of a temple differs considerably from that of a present-day synagogue, church or mosque. These are all, first and foremost, places of congregation, meeting places for the faithful, where they assemble to pray and study their sacred books. A temple, on the other hand, was the place where the deity lived and often his or her followers were not even allowed inside the building. That was a privilege reserved for the priests.

According to the scriptures the temple built by Solomon for the god of Israel was one such 'dwelling'. It is stated literally in the Bible, that the king had built a 'house for the Lord' (2 Chronicles 7:11). The deity was present in the temple, in the 'Holy of Holies', into which only the high priest was allowed to enter and only on one day in the year: the Day of Atonement.

Solomon's temple had other functions too. It was the place where sacrificial services were conducted, involving oblations, incense offerings and burnt offerings and where animals were sacrificed. These services usually took place on the forecourt

Figure 11.1 Solomon with the plan of the temple by Jean-Baptiste Despax, 18th century (Toulouse Cathedral, CC BY-SA 4.0).

rather than in the building itself. The sacrificial rites were accompanied by specific prayers. The faithful received the priestly blessing, the words of which can still be found in Numbers 6:24–28: 'The Lord bless you and keep you; the Lord make His face shine upon you, and be gracious to you; the Lord turn his face toward you and give you peace.'

The temple complex was also a place of instruction in the stories and laws of the people; it was a court of law and a place of refuge. If you had accidentally killed somebody, you could escape revenge by fleeing into the temple courtyard and grasping the horns of the altar. Sometimes the temple also functioned as the national 'treasury', where money was collected for national enterprises, such as the army in case of war.

History of the Jerusalem temple

According to the biblical narrative (see below) king Solomon built the temple in Jerusalem with the aid of Phoenician artisans. The building of the temple is usually dated about 965 BC, according to the biblical chronology explained in Chapter 5, and this temple stood until its destruction by the Babylonian king Nebuchadnezzar in 587 BC – altogether a little less than 400 years. Unfortunately nothing has ever been found of this building, so it is impossible to verify either date. This building is known as the 'first temple'.

An inscription, found in 2001, sent shockwaves through the world (at least the world of the faithful), as it described repairs to the temple by king Jehoash, proving beyond doubt that the first temple had really existed. Unfortunately the inscription seems to be a forgery (see below).

After the Persians conquered the Neo-Babylonian empire in 539 BC the Jewish exiles obtained permission from king Cyrus I to return to Jerusalem and rebuild the temple (Ezra 1:1–4). The first group of Judaeans started on the long journey home, led by Sesbazzar or Zerubbabel (the text is not entirely clear). The temple furniture, carried off to Babylonia by king Nebuchadnezzar Ii almost 50 years earlier, was returned to them (Ezra 1:8). When they arrived in Jerusalem they found the town and the temple in ruins. It was only years later, around 520 BC, that they started to erect a new temple (Ezra 5). Under the circumstances it is likely that this temple was a fairly simple building; it is known as the 'second temple'. No remains of this building have ever been found either.

When Herod the Great gained power in 37 BC, this 'second temple' had stood for almost 500 years and was in desperate need of reconstruction. Herod decided to build a completely new temple. This building is also known as the 'second temple' (even though it is really the third one). It was finally destroyed by the Romans in 70 AD.

Ever since its final destruction, plans have been made to rebuild the Jerusalem temple – that would officially be the 'third temple'. The first plan was hatched by the

Byzantine emperor and successor of Constantine the Great, Julian the Apostate, who reigned AD 361–363. He gave instructions to rebuild the 'second temple', but these plans were never executed. Today various groups of pious Jews are actively making preparations for the building of a new temple, which would be constructed on the platform that now holds the al-Aqsa Mosque and the Dome of the Rock.

Solomon's temple as described in the Bible

The Bible gives two descriptions of the temple itself (in 1 Kings 6 and 7:13–51 and in 2 Chronicles 3 and 4). These descriptions show that the temple was a rectangular building, measuring 30 × 10 m and 15 m in height, and that it was oriented east–west (Fig. 11.2).

It had a tripartite internal division. The first section was a narrow forecourt fronted by two 'copper' pillars, over 10 m high, which were named Jakin and Boaz. The central part (the Holy) had floors of cypress wood and walls of cedar, which were covered in gold. Here stood an altar of cedar wood, also covered in gold, which

Figure 11.2 Sixteenth century gravure of a reconstruction of the temple of Solomon (detail) by Francisco Vatablo (Biblical Museum, Amsterdam, public domain).

served to burn incense, as well as the 'table on which was the showbread', and ten golden lamp stands, each with seven lamps. The final room, the Holy of Holies, was smaller and narrower: 10 × 10 × 10 m. It contained the Ark of the Covenant which had accompanied the Israelites on their journey through the desert (Exodus 25:10–22). On top of the Ark were two giant cherubim, each standing 5 m high and also covered in gold. This room was shrouded in darkness, because of the presence of the deity.

Surrounding the temple building were two walled forecourts. The inner court was reserved for the priests. It contained a large sacrificial altar, made of bronze, with horns on its corners, and the 'Sea of Bronze', a bronze water vessel with a diameter of 5 m, carried by 12 bronze bulls. The outer forecourt was for the common people. Here lavers were found, water basins for washing sacrificial animals, cooking vessels, shovels and water carts. Many of these furnishings were made of gold.

According to the biblical description, the interior of the temple was also completely covered in gold. The exterior was decorated with stone sculptures of cherubim, palm trees and flower buds. It took 7 years to build the temple – whereas, as 1 Kings 7:1 disapprovingly remarks, Solomon spent 13 years on the building of his own palace. This palace and the palace Solomon built for his wife, the daughter of the pharaoh, were located near the temple.

Other gods

There were times when the temple had other 'occupants' than the god of Israel. The gods Baal and Asherah were venerated in the temple but other 'foreign' deities in the shape of the sun, the moon and the stars were found there as well. When king Josiah started a religious reform he had to remove all sorts of objects dedicated to these gods. The biblical text speaks of 'furnishings' for these gods, of a 'sacred pole' in the temple itself and of the 'booths' for male prostitutes on the forecourt, where women were weaving covers for the Asherah statues. The king also removed the horses that were dedicated to the sun, and a sun-chariot by the entrance to the temple, as well as altars on the roof and on the two forecourts (2 Kings 23:1–14).

Assuming that these words describe a real, existing situation, the gods venerated originated in the Phoenician pantheon, chiefly Baal and Asherah, and in Mesopotamia, such as the sun, the moon and the stars, and the horses dedicated to the sun. These would be part of the cult of the sun god, with his sun-chariot drawn by four horses.

Ezekiel the prophet who, in 597 BC, had been exiled to Babylon together with thousands of other high ranking Judaeans, describes a vision he received concerning the excesses taking place in the temple. (this was before the destruction of the temple by the Babylonians in 587 BC). Ezekiel 8:14 says: 'Then he brought me to the entrance of the north gate of the house of the Lord, and I saw women sitting there, mourning the god Tammuz.' According to the biblical scholar Meindert Dijkstra we should read: 'THE women ... weeping for Tammuz' – which is also what it literally says in the Hebrew text. According to Dijkstra this refers to a caste of cult personnel, the *qedesim*, which also included women. The veneration of Tammuz appears to have been an established element of the temple cult. Tammuz is also the name of one of the months of the Jewish calendar. It is probably named after the same month in the Babylonian calendar, which was named after the god Tammuz.

What has been found of the temple?

Whether Solomon's temple was really as rich and beautiful as the stories convey is something we will never know. Nothing, not a single stone, has been found of this temple. It was destroyed when the Babylonians conquered Jerusalem in 586 BC. The Babylonians took the gold that remained – much of it had already disappeared as tribute payments to Egypt and Assyria – and burned down the building.

An inscription has been found in Arad,that may contain a reference to the temple in Jerusalem. The ostracon is part of the archive of the commander of the Arad fortress and is dated around 600 BC. The end of one of his letters says:

> And concerning the matter about which you
> commanded me, it is well.
> He is staying in the house of YHWH.

a

b

The 'house of YHWH' may refer to the temple in Jerusalem, although, since there was also a temple in Arad (see below), the commander may have meant that temple. We do not know who the person was who stayed in the house of YHWH.

One object that may be connected to the Jerusalem temple is an ivory pomegranate. During excavations on the Temple Mount in 1979 this object was discovered in an antique shop in Jerusalem. It disappeared before it could be acquired. Years later it surfaced in Switzerland and, through an anonymous donor, came into the possession of the Israel Museum. The pomegranate is 4.3 cm high and may have been used as the finial of a sceptre or stave (Fig. 11.3a). It bears an engraved inscription in ancient Hebrew script, which says (in translation): 'Property of the House of the Lord, sacred to the priests' (Fig. 11.3b). The function of the sceptre is unclear. The pomegranate is a well-known symbol in the Bible. It was used extensively in the building of the temple (1 Kings 7:18–20), while the robe of

Figure 11.3 a. Ivory pomegranate (www.BibleLandPictures.com/Alamy Stock Photo); b. inscription on ivory pomegranate (Wikikati, public domain).

the high priest was decorated with pomegranates (Exodus 28:33). Unfortunately this inscription also seems to be a forgery (see below).

Location of the Temple

Because nothing has been found of the temple that was allegedly built by Solomon we cannot be certain where it would have been located. The Bible calls the spot where Solomon started building 'Mount Moriah, where the Lord had appeared to his father David. It was on the threshing floor of Araunah the Jebusite' (2 Chronicles 3:1). This will have been the hilltop north of the City of David, the present Haram esh-Sharif or Temple Mount, and it must have been a good location for a threshing floor once because it caught the wind. It has been suggested that here, next to the threshing floor, had stood a local Canaanite sanctuary which made it a suitable spot for a new temple.

Presently the top of Temple Mount is covered by a large platform, built by Herod the Great, on which two beautiful Islamic sanctuaries are located: the al-Aqsa Mosque and the Dome of the Rock (Fig. 11.4). It is generally assumed that the temple stood on the spot where now the Dome of the Rock stands, that with its golden dome it is certainly a worthy successor in terms of magnificence.

Figure 11.4 The Haram esh-Sharif or Temple Mount in Jerusalem (Andrew Shiva, CC BY-SA 4.0).

Many scholars think that the Holy of Holies of the temple was built on top of the rock which is now the central point in the Dome of the Rock. Others believe that the rock itself was used as a place of sacrifice and that the temple stood to the north of it. A location to the south of the rock has also been suggested. Arguments have been brought forward for each suggestion, but none of these arguments are (naturally) based on remains of the actual temple. It is generally assumed that the entrance of the temple was on the east side, a common feature in Ancient Near Eastern temples. However, not everybody locates the temple on the Temple Mount. There is a (persistent) trend to place the temple inside the City of David, so to the south of the Temple Mount. No traces of a temple have been found there either.

A myth?

Let us return to the questions asked at the beginning of this chapter. Why is it so difficult to find remains of this temple? Did it actually exist at all? Did Solomon really build it, and if so, where was it located? Or is the whole thing in fact a myth?

Personally, I do not think the stories concerning the temple are a myth. Nearly every Ancient Near Eastern city had a temple, and the capital of a state housed the most magnificent temple of all, dedicated to the city god(dess) or to the supreme national deity. We can therefore take for granted that there was a temple for YHWH in Jerusalem, particularly since a large part of the biblical narrative is situated around the temple.

When exactly the temple was built, by whom, and what it looked like, are questions that are not so easy to answer. Solomon could have been the builder, if only we had clear evidence of his existence. As explained in Chapter 5, Solomon himself is problematic. It seems more likely that the temple dated from the 9th century BC, the time when cities were built in Judah and Israel, and royal authority was established and/or stabilised.

That nothing has been found of the temple is not as strange as it may seem. It was destroyed by the Babylonians, rebuilt after the Exile, and finally completely renovated on a grand scale by king Herod. Herod had the old temple dismantled stone by stone, and the builders no doubt reused these stones for the new building, thereby removing all traces of the old one (see below).

Herod's temple in Jerusalem

To complete the story, let us cast a quick look at Herod's temple and its sorrowful fate. When Herod the Great came to power in 37 BC he decided to build a new temple, a temple that would outshine all Roman building projects in the southern Levant. In order to do that, he created a new temple platform, twice as large as the old one, with a surface of about 14 ha. When the preliminary preparations were finished the old temple was dismantled. Thousands of workers were employed and within 18 months a new building was erected. The completion of the whole temple complex, however, would take several decades. According to Flavius Josephus, the Jewish historian, the king started preparations for the building of the temple in the 18th year of his reign, around 20 BC. The temple was inaugurated 10 years later. But the complex as a whole was not finished until AD 64 – just a few years before the destruction of the city by the Romans. This is the temple that Jesus visited and out of which he drove the money changers (Matthew 21:21–17).

We find the most extensive descriptions of the new temple in the works of Flavius Josephus, dated to the 1st century AD, and in the tractate Middoth, from the fifth book of the Mishnah, a collection of Jewish religious laws dated to the beginning of the 3rd century AD. There is no description of the temple in the New Testament.

The new building matched Solomon's temple in size and likewise consisted of three sections: a forecourt, the main sanctuary (the 'Holy') and, at the back, the 'Holy of Holies' (Fig. 11.5). The forecourt was wider than the rest of the sanctuary and was connected to the Holy through double gold-plated doors. A heavy curtain, embroidered in Babylonian style, hung before the doors. According to Josephus three artworks, all made of gold, stood in the sanctuary: the Menorah (the lampstand with seven branches), the table of the showbread, and an incense altar. In the Holy of Holies, separated from the Holy by only a curtain, the Ark of the Covenant stood no longer, but a flattened stone, called the 'foundation stone' was laid; it was supposed to connect earth and heaven. Nobody was allowed to enter or even see this space, except the High Priest, once a year, on the Day of Atonement. The building was constructed in marble, and the walls, inside as well as outside, were partly covered with sheets of gold. Flavius Josephus wrote that 'he who has not seen the (temple) building of Herod, has never seen a beautiful building in his life'.

Figure 11.5 Reconstruction of Herod's temple in the Israel Museum, Jerusalem (photo: Berthold Werner, public domain).

Compared to the temple complex built by Solomon, there was a greater distinction between the sacred and the profane. There were no longer any palaces on the temple grounds. The temple itself was surrounded by three courts: the outer 'court of the gentiles', which was open to everybody; then there was a 'court for the (Jewish) women', while the innermost court was the 'court of the Israelites', where only Jewish men including priests were allowed. The great altar for burnt offerings stood in this court.

Most scholars agree that the temple stood on the giant platform commissioned by Herod the Great. Exactly where on this platform it stood is unknown, because, again, nothing has been found of the temple building itself. The most likely location is where now the Dome of the Rock stands.

The destruction

The year AD 66 saw the outbreak of the First Jewish revolt, which has been extensively recorded by Josephus in his book *The Jewish War*. The temple complex played a major part during the siege of Jerusalem by the Romans. The temple grounds were occupied by various groups of Zealots, in combat with each other: a group headed by John of Giscala controlled the temple square while another group, that of Eleazar ben Simon, had occupied the temple itself and the inner court. The temple was conquered by the Roman army who set fire to it on the 9th day of the month of Av (which is still a Jewish day of mourning). Titus, the Roman general, returned to Rome taking with him the menorah and the table of the showbreads, as depicted on the triumphal arch which was erected in his honour in Rome. The temple would never be rebuilt.

What has been found of this temple?

Until recently, the only known remains of the second temple consisted of the terrace on which it had been built. This terrace measured 300 × 500 m and its height at the southern end was 55 m. The terrace was built in typical Herodian style, recognisable by the use of very large dressed stones with a slightly protruding rusticated surface surrounded by a flat edge. The majority of the stones were 3–4 m long and 1 m high; the longest is 12 m long and weighs many tons. The Wailing Wall is part of the western support wall of this terrace, so it is not part of the temple itself.

Excavations on the outside of the temple terrace have been going on since 1968 and have uncovered many remains of buildings and objects that once stood on the temple terrace. At the southern end of the terrace, where now the al-Aqsa mosque stands, was once a beautifully decorated colonnade, the 'royal stoa'. The temple square could be accessed through a system of staircases, bridges and underground passageways, many parts of which have been found during the archaeological excavations. A discussion of all these excavations would go too far here. You can find further information in the recommended reading at the end of this book.

An interesting find was a stone with an inscription. The (not quite complete) text consisted of the Hebrew characters L B T H T K I 'H L H CH. This can be translated as 'to the place of trumpeting to [call out]'. Josephus informs us that it was custom to blow the 'shofar', the ramshorn, from one of the towers of the temple square, on the evenings of the 6th and 7th day of the week, in order to announce the beginning and end of the shabbat. Possibly this stone indicated the place where the horn was blown.

So, even though remains of Herod's temple complex have been found, particularly of the access routes and bridges on the outside, the temple itself is gone completely. One can assume that the stones have been reused for other buildings.

Other temples for the god of Israel

Many text in the Bible emphasise that only one temple for the god of Israel existed: the temple in Jerusalem. YHWH could only be venerated in the Holy City. However, other biblical texts seem to hint at the existence of other sanctuaries, although most have not (yet?) been found in archaeological excavations. Surprisingly, several temples for the God of Israel have been excavated outside of Jerusalem and on all of these the Bible is silent. Furthermore, extra-biblical texts refer to two temples located in Egypt which have not yet been found. A short overview of this intriguing situation is given here.

Temples hinted at in the biblical texts

According to 1 Kings 12:28–30 Jeroboam, king of the norther kingdom of Israel, set up golden calves in Bethel and in Dan, two important border towns.

> After seeking advice, the king made two golden calves. He said to the people, 'It is too much for you to go up to Jerusalem. Here are your gods, Israel, who brought you up out of Egypt.' One he set up in Bethel, and the other in Dan. And this thing became a sin; the people came to worship the one at Bethel and went as far as Dan to worship the other.

These young bulls were thus seen as the symbol of the god YHWH, which is ironic because in the biblical narrative around Moses, the golden calf the Hebrews set up in de desert, was perceived as an idol invoking the wrath of the Lord (Exodus 32). Most scholars think that the bulls were pedestals on which the (invisible) god was standing, as was the case with many statues of a god in the ancient Near East. As Jeroboam 'set up' these bulls in Dan and Bethel, one may assume he built shrines or temples there. Excavations at Bethel which name, interestingly, means 'house of god', have uncovered nothing of the sort; archaeological work at Dan, however, did yield a large sanctuary. No golden bull, eilas, was found therein. For the excavated shrine at Dan, see below.

Another temple with a golden calf is hinted at in Hosea 8:4–5, this time in Samaria, the capital of the northern kingdom. The prophet Hosea reports on the anger of YHWH who says: 'With their silver and gold they make idols for themselves to their own destruction. Samaria, throw out your calf-idol! My anger burns against them.' Samaria has been excavated, but no temple has been found there (see Chapter 6).

Temples excavated in ancient Israel

A temple has been excavated at Arad in Israel, while a large opn-air sanctuary was uncovered in Dan. Recently a temple was found at Tel Motza, near Jerusalem. These three complexes all date to the Late Iron Age. On Mount Gerizim, near Samaria, a temple was erected by the Samaritans, in the Persian period.

Cult place at Tel Dan

At Tel Dan in the north of ancient Israel, a large open-air cult place has been uncovered (Fig. 11.6). It consists of a walled enclosure measuring 45 × 60 m, containing a stone-built altar next to a large stone podium of roughly 18 × 19 m. The podium was either an open-air offering place or *bamah*, or it may have functioned as the base for a temple. No temple walls were, however, found. Both structures were made of nicely cut stones called 'ashlars'. Cultic vessels were plentiful as well as thousands of animal bones,

Figure 11.6 The Cult place at Tel Dan (בורמ רמת Pikiwiki IsraeCC BY 2.5).

remains of either burnt offerings or of feasting: a ritual in which meat is dispensed among the believers for a communal meal. The excavators date the complex to the 10th–8th centuries BC.

It is assumed that this sacred complex was dedicated to YHWH, as Dan was part of the kingdom of Israel according to biblical texts, but no statues of a god or inscriptions mentioning a deity were found. As described above, king Jeroboam set up a golden calf in Dan.

Temple in Arad

The only Iron Age temple building found in Judah stood in Arad in the Negev desert. The Bible, ironically, does not mention this temple. It was a rectangular building, measuring about 15 × 10 m. Like the Jerusalem temple, it had a tripartite layout: a court, a main sanctuary (the 'Holy') and a back room (the 'Holy of Holies'). In the back room was a raised platform on which stood two steles with traces of red paint. They may have been symbols of the deity (or deities). In this room two incense altars were found.

In the forecourt of the temple a large altar for burnt offerings was built, measuring 2.5 × 2.5 m, and made of mudbricks and uncut stones. The temple was part of a large fortress which guarded a trade route (Fig. 11.7). The fortress was in use from roughly

Figure 11.7 Reconstruction of the fortress at Arad. The small temple is located at the right upper corner of the drawing (Mboesch, CC BY-SA 4.0).

the 10th to the 6th century BC. Since Arad was in Judah, it is generally assumed that the temple was dedicated to YHWH, although no inscriptions of any kind have been found. The ostracon discussed above, with its reference to the 'house of YHWH', could refer not only to the temple in Jerusalem but also to this temple, but that is by no means certain.

Tel Motza temple

About 7 km north-west of Jerusalem a large temple complex has been partially excavated during construction work for a new road to the city. In the Iron Age Tel Motza was a small town seemingly specialising in grain produce and storage. The temple consisted of a long building established on an east–west axis with thick walls and stone pillar bases. A stone altar for burnt offerings, 1.35 × 1.4 m in size, was erected in the courtyard. A refuse pit was discovered beside it, filled with pottery sherds, animal bones and ashes, probably the remains of sacrifices made on the altar. A small stone podium was situated nearby and several cultic objects were found in the area between pit and podium, among which four figurines, a large decorated and several undecorated cult stands.

The temple dates to the 9th–8th centuries BC. A large building was constructed over it in the 7th century BC but it is unclear if this was a temple too. Located so near to Jerusalem, one may assume that this temple was dedicated to the god of Israel and not another deity. It is interesting that this temple functioned so close to the temple in Jerusalem itself.

The temple of the Samaritans

Israel, the northern Kingdom, had been conquered by the Assyrians in 722 BC, some 150 years before the fall of Judah in 587 BC. The Assyrians had exiled a large part of the original population and had replaced them with immigrants from other conquered lands and regions. One may assume that the part of the original population that had not been exiled, still prayed to the God of Israel, and considered themselves to be Israelites. It is also very possible that some of the immigrants began to venerated the local deity.

However when, after the Exile, the Judeans returned to their homeland, from 539 BC onwards, they rejected the inhabitants of the region of Samaria, located between the Galilee in the north and Judah in the south, as real 'Jews'. They felt the same, incidentally, about those Judaeans who had not been exiled but had remained in Judah, and their offspring. The texts on the original inhabitants of the land and their offer to help rebuild the temple in Jerusalem are found in Ezra 4, about the exclusion of 'foreign women' in Ezra 10, and about the veneration of YHWH by immigrant peoples in 2 Kings 17:24–41.

According to Flavius Josephus, the Samaritans, rejected by the community of Jews in Judah, now built their own temple in Samaria, on Mount Gerizim, in the

5th century BC. Their temple conformed to the measurements of the ancient Jerusalem temple, of which it was the successor, and it was dedicated to YHWH. A stone has been found with the tetragram YHWH engraved in it. This temple was destroyed in the 2nd century BC.

Excavations were conducted on Mount Gerizim in 1960–64 and 1982–2004. Parts of the temple area were excavated but a ground plan of the temple has not been recovered, possibly because Herod the Great had a large temple dedicated to the Roman gods built over its ruins. In the much later Byzantine era, a church was built on the spot. The whole area is now an archaeological park.

The temple has been depicted on some coins, dated to the 3rd and 2nd centuries

Figure 11.8 Coin showing the temple at Samaria on top of Mount Gerizim with steps leading up to it. At the foot of the hill a pillared hall is visible (public domain).

BC, minted in Neapolis (the 'new town' that was built over ancient Samaria). The coins shows Mount Gerizim with the temple on top (Fig. 11.8). Steps lead up to the temple and a colonnade is visible at the foot of the mountain. Modern-day Samaritans still live in the vicinity of Mount Gerizim and perform their rituals there.

Temples in Egypte

In Egypt two temples dedicated to the god of Israel have been documented. Excavations have not yet revealed them.

The tempel at Elephantine

Elephantine is an island in the Nile, in the south of Egypt, where a number of papyri from the Persian period have been found. In this period (around 550–400 BC) Elephantine housed a military colony, in which mercenaries from Judah were also stationed. These mercenaries, who spoke Aramaic, built a temple there dedicated to their god Yaho or Yo. The temple itself has not been found but the papyri, consisting of letters and contracts, paint a lively picture of the life and the activities going on in the garrison and the temple. Around 400 BC the garrison was dismantled and the soldiers left.

Based on descriptions in the papyri a reconstruction of the temple has been attempted: a small shrine standing in an open courtyard with an altar for animal sacrifices (Fig. 11.9). Nothing as grand as the temples in Jerusalem or on Mount Gerizim, but a temple nonetheless.

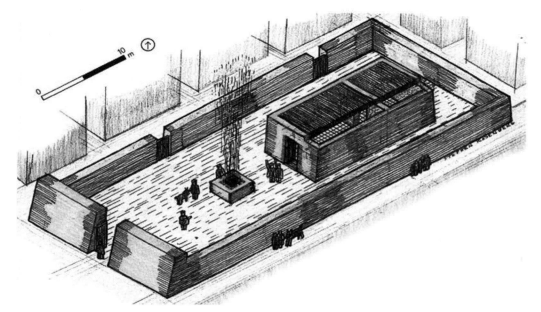

Figure 11.9 Reconstruction of the temple at Elephantine (Stephen G. Rosenberg).

The temple of Onias

Another Jewish temple ostensibly was located in Leontopolis, north of present-day Cairo in Egypt. This temple was described twice by Josephus. In his book *Jewish Antiquities,* he states that the temple looked like the temple in Jerusalem, but in *The Jewish War* he describes it as looking like a fortress, with towers 30 m high. According to him this temple was built by a certain Onias. In the Hellenistic era there were several high priests in Jerusalem named Onias. Onias IV, so says Josephus, was expelled by another high priest named Jason and fled to Egypt, which event would have taken place in about 170 BC. Here he obtained permission from Pharaoh Ptolemais IV to erect a temple in Leontopolis. Onias brought with him an army which assisted the Pharaoh in protecting the border with Palestine. Eventually the temple was destroyed by the Romans in AD 73.

Leontopolis is located at Tell el-Yehudiyeh ('the mound of the Jew'), excavated by Sir Flinders Petrie in the beginning of the 20th century. Most of his finds dated to the Bronze Age. Of course, he looked also for Onias' temple as described by Josephus. In an article in *The Jerusalem Post* on 10 July, 2008, Stephen Rosenberg, writes:[3]

> In early 1906 the famous Egyptologist Sir William Flinders Petrie spent six weeks at a site called Tel el-Yehudiyeh and claimed he had found the Temple of Onias, on a sandy mound attached to the city of Rameses III. Because of the great Jewish interest, he gave a lecture on it at King's College in London, which was reported in the Jewish Chronicle of May 18, 1906. He had made a model of the temple, which was like the towered fortress described by Josephus, and he invited all present to view it at

University College. The British chief rabbi of the time, Hermann Adler, thanked Petrie for his great discovery and service to the Jewish community. Unfortunately Petrie's model has disappeared and so has the original site.

In other words, nothing is left of the temple, neither of the original, nor of the model.

Forged inscriptions

Recently an inscription related to the temple in Jerusalem has turned out to be a forgery. It is not the first forged inscription nor will it be the last. The hunger for 'real' objects related to Ancient Israel and especially its temple, is so great, that it creates a market. There will always be sellers to accommodate the demand. As the ability to discover forgeries grows, with the implementation of sophisticated analyses, so does the skill of the forgers. The tale recounted below serves as an illustration of how difficult it is to unmask a forgery and as a warning not to be too receptive of discoveries that are heralded too loudly.

The story of the discovery and exposure of this particular object has all the characteristics of a bad thriller: secretive meetings, a private detective with a briefcase, man hunts, a grieving widow, big money, police raids, a secret workshop, a court case and an unexpected ending. But this is a real-life thriller.

The discovery

In the summer of 2001 a secret meeting takes place somewhere in Jerusalem. A professor from Hebrew University receives a mysterious phone call from a man who introduces himself as a private detective. He has brought a briefcase which he opened with a dramatic gesture, to reveal a dark grey stone carrying an inscription. The inscription is in ancient Hebrew – the language spoken and written in the days of the Hebrew Bible. Large inscriptions from that period have rarely been found in Israel. This one did not stem from a regular excavation but belonged to someone whose name was not to be revealed.

To authenticate the inscription, the seller contacts the Israeli Geological Institute, a renowned research institute. Two of its researchers analyse the stone, the patina on the stone and in the individual letters, and carbon particles in the patina. Patina is a coloured film on the surface of stone or metal objects, produced by oxidation over a long period. It gives a clue to the age of the objects. They conclude that the stone is a local sandstone and the patina covers all of the stone and continues in the individual letters of the inscription, so both the stone and the inscription are old. The patina contains chemical elements that are present in Jerusalem. In other words: the inscription is genuine. Radiocarbon dating places the carbon particles in the 3rd century BC, which means that the inscription must be older. Finally they discover that there are gold particles present in the patina.

What is so special about this stone? The inscription refers to the temple of Solomon. Biblical text put it the temple was built around 965 BC by king Solomon, as described above. About 100 years later king Jehoash had the temple repaired. 2 Kings 12:4–5 says:

> Joash said to the priests, Collect all the money that is brought as sacred offerings to the temple of the LORD—the money collected in the census, the money received from personal vows and the money brought voluntarily to the temple. Let every priest receive the money from one of the treasurers, then use it to repair whatever damage is found in the temple.

Below is the text of the inscription (the first lines are damaged and difficult to decipher):

> [I am Yeho'ash, son of A]hazyahu, k[ing over Ju]dah, and I executed the re[pai]rs. When men's hearts became replete with generosity in the land and in the steppe, and in all the cities of Judah, to donate money for the sacred contributions abundantly, in order to purchase quarry stone and juniper wood and Edomite copper/copper from (the city of) 'Adam, (and) in order to perform the work faithfully, – (then) I renovated the breach(es) of the Temple and of the surrounding walls, and the storied structure, and the mesh-work, and the winding stairs, and the recesses, and the doors. May (this inscribed stone) become this day a witness that the work has succeeded (and) may God (thus) ordain His people with a blessing.

In other words, according to the inscription, king Jehoash succeeded in collecting the money and he completed the repairs. The name of the king himself, incidentally, is missing, only the name 'Ahazyahu' is still readable. This king, therefore, was a son of Ahazyahu, and that can only be Jehoash, who reigned 836–797 BC, according to the biblical chronology explained in Chapter 1.

So, here was proof that the temple existed in the 9th century BC and needed repairs. In other words, it must have been built much earlier. The inscription confirms the story of the building of the temple by Solomon and the repairs by Jehoash. An interesting detail is that the gold particles are thought to have precipitated on the stone in 587 BC, when the temple was destroyed by the Neo-Babylonians in a great conflagration. The temple, after all, had been covered in gold.

A few months later the inscription is published receives a sceptical response from the scholarly community. Archaeologists wonder where the stone was found. It does not come from a regular excavation which, in itself, makes the discovery suspect. Linguists have other suspicions. The individual letters are written in different writing styles, something that is very unusual in official inscriptions. Some words are not used correctly and the spelling of some words is modern.

Notwithstanding these objections, now that the stone has been declared genuine by the Geological Institute (autumn 2001) the Israel Museum in Jerusalem, the largest archaeological museum in Israel, becomes interested. The private detective negotiates with the museum on behalf of the owner (who still wishes to remain anonymous), and according to those in the know they are discussing a sum of 3– 10 million dollars. But the museum first wants to see the stone and to know its provenance, that is, it wants to know where the stone was found.

But now, suddenly, the stone disappears together with the detective and his briefcase. It takes 9 months to trace him and he confesses that he is commissioned by a well-known businessman and collector of antiquities. The collector claims that he is not the owner of the stone. He represents a Palestinian antiques dealer who has, by now, passed away. His widow lives, together with the stone, deep in the Palestinian Territories and cannot be contacted or reached because of the intifada, the uprising of the Palestinians. However, the man claims to know where the stone was found: close to the Temple Mount, which would confirm the authenticity of the stone.

Figure 11.10 The James ossuary. It was on display at the Royal Ontario Museum from November 15, 2002 to January 5, 2003 (https://commons.wikimedia.org/wiki/File:JamesOssuary-1-.jpg).

A second inscription

At that point the story takes a remarkable twist. Around the same time, in October 2002, a second sensational inscription is presented to the world, by the same collector of antiquities! He had an antique ossuary which stood on his balcony, with plants in it. An ossuary is a stone chest that was used in antiquity to contain the bones of deceased people (Fig. 11.10). Most of these ossuaries date to the Roman era and they are found in large quantities. Some bear an inscription with the name of the deceased, most do not. By sheer coincidence, this ossuary does have an inscription, something the collector had failed to notice earlier – and not just any inscription ...

The carving in the side panel of the chest reads: 'James, son of Joseph, brother of Jesus'. This find causes a major sensation. Here was the physical evidence of the existence of Jesus of Nazareth. An epigraphist with an established reputation examines the chest and declares the inscription genuine. He dates it to the period between 20 BC and AD 70. Experts from the Geological Institute who had examined the Jehoash inscription, also examine the chest and declare the patina to be old. The American journal *Biblical Archaeology Review* organises a major publicity campaign. The story is taken up by all major newspapers, *Discovery Channel* produces a documentary and a book is published about the find. In November 2002 the ossuary is flown to Toronto, where a major archaeological and biblical conference is taking place. In Toronto the chest is exhibited at the museum, where it is admired by some 100,000 visitors, myself among them.

Various reputed scholars vouch for the authenticity of the inscription (at least for its antiquity), but still it evokes mixed reactions. For many people the whole thing is just a bit too convenient. An experienced collector of antiquities owning such a clear and obvious inscription without realising it? An ossuary mentioning not only the name of the deceased and his father, but also his brother? The name of Joseph as the father of Jesus, on a first century chest, while the oldest gospels never mention his name?

So when, a few months later, the discovery of the Jehoash inscription is made public, scepticism prevails. Here is the same collector who offers for sale two inscriptions, almost at the same time, both of which are the kind of inscriptions the world has been yearning for: a literal confirmation of the biblical stories. Many people think it too good to be true. The Israeli authorities agree. They raid the collector's house and storerooms and find not only the stone with the Jehoash inscription – which was supposedly unattainably hidden in the Palestinian Territories – but also the ossuary, now returned from Toronto.

New investigations

So now the Israeli authorities have the two inscribed objects in their possession and it is time to find out whether they are genuine or forgeries. They bring together 14 scholars and experts: biblical scholars, archaeologists, linguists, petrographists and physicists. One team examines the physical properties of the inscription (the stone and patina, the way the letters were made), the other team concentrates on the language of the inscriptions.

In the end, both teams agree that the objects themselves (both the stone and the ossuary) are genuine and old. However, based on many observations, the inscriptions are not. For the Jehoash inscription they conclude that it cannot be an old text but has to be a forgery made on an old stone plaque. The text on the ossuary is partly old ('brother of Jesus' – Jesus being a common name in that period), partly new ('James, son of Joseph'). Of course, some scholars disagree with the two teams and maintain that the anomalies and inconsistencies can be explained in other ways, but the finds have lost not only their glitter but also their credibility and are not exhibited anywhere.

Not the end

When the conclusions of the research are made known ('forgeries'), the Israeli police conduct another raid on the collector's property and now they discover a secret workshop with a complete toolkit for the production of 'antique' objects, such as different kinds of stone, tools and electric drills. They also find several partly finished objects: royal seals and a mould for a bronze statue. The collector is taken into custody, and confesses to having sold forged antiquities for about 15 years. Many of these objects have been bought by museums and collectors. Afterwards he retracts his confession; he is completely innocent.

A court case starts for which 138 experts are consulted and which takes years to conclude. The experts do not agree with each other, driving the judges into despair. In 2012 the court decides that the Israel Antiquity Authorities has not legally proven that the objects are forgeries (although the judges concede that they can neither rule that they are genuine) and the collector and his associates are acquitted of most charges. The stone and the ossuary have to be returned to him. Notwithstanding this court ruling, for most scholars the scientific verdict ('forgeries') surpasses the legal verdict ('not proven').

Another forgery disclosed

In the last week of December 2004 the affair again hits the headlines. Museums all over the world have by now begun to check their inventory and to test their objects. The small ivory pomegranate discussed above, which carries an inscription, also turns out to be a fake. The object was discovered in 1979 in an antique shop in Jerusalem. The inscription reads: 'Sacred to the priests in the house of God'. The pomegranate was considered to be the only object ever recovered that had belonged to the 'first temple' in Jerusalem. It was bought in 1988 by the Israel Museum, who paid almost 1 million dollars for it, and was one of the highlights of the exhibition. Now it turns out that the pomegranate itself was ancient, dating from the Late Bronze Age. The inscription, on the other hand, has been inscribed recently and is thus a forgery. The museum removes the object from its place of honour.

Aftermath

The aftermath of the whole affair is immense. It is possible that many archaeological objects that have been bought by museums in the last decades are forgeries. Several of the objects have by now been investigated and proven to be fakes. But how many are still being exhibited in the museums in Jerusalem, in London, New York or Paris?

Worse: the forgers have exploited the desires of millions of Christians and Jews who want proof that the Bible is true, that the stories told are historical facts. But the only result of this giant forging operation is that those who were not believers in the first place, are now more sceptical than ever. What seemed too good to be true, turned out to be just that. Whoever will still believe that the next discovery is genuine?

Note

1 http://www.jpost.com/Magazine/Features/The-papyrus-path.

Epilogue

So many Bible stories, so many excavations and finds, so many inscriptions, and so many different opinions and interpretations. Is the reader of this book now able to 'read' the biblical stories in the light of the results of excavations? Or to relate the archaeological finds to the information extracted from the Bible? Probably not, but maybe this has been made clear: biblical verses and archaeological finds cannot simply be superimposed. Results from excavations cannot and do not confirm stories from the Bible, if only because archaeology's research aim is completely different from the Bible's meaning.

Archaeological research sets out to find traces of the people inhabiting the land and from that deduce the social, economic, religious and political systems in which they lived. And yes, sometimes it is possible to glimpse their historical development. The Bible's meaning is not to describe the lives of the peoples and the history of their kingdoms but to show how God intervened in those lives and histories. The stories were once written down to communicate this central idea, not to be 'true'. That does not mean that no historically reliable components are present in the stories; it means that archaeology and Bible approach the ancient land and its people from completely different angles. Sometimes they converge and often they do not.

In the best of times, excavation results can provide a picture of the tangible situation 'on the ground', of the living conditions in the region in which the biblical stories are set. And – sometimes – the biblical stories can give insight into the thoughts and feelings of the people living in the Iron Age, even if these stories have been written down long after the fact.

I hope that after reading this book the reader will take a step back when hearing once again that archaeology confirms the Bible, that this time an excavated inscription really proves that David slew Goliath, or that archaeologists have found the palace of queen Jezebel. I hope that s/he – with me – thinks: 'No friends, that is not what archaeology does and can do. The relationship between archaeology and the Bible is much more complicated that you are presenting here. Show me what you have really found, and I will go and investigate.'

Further reading

In addition to relevant books and articles I am including references to websites with reliable information. I am aware that websites change, are deleted or given new names. However, with so much information freely and easily available on the internet it seems pointless not to use these sources. If a website is not available anymore, please search for comparable websites on the same subject.

Chapter 1

Various translations of the Bible are to be found at Bible Gateway: www.biblegateway.com/.

Dever, W. 2017. *Beyond the Texts: An Archaeological Portrait of Ancient Israel and Judah*. Society of Biblical Literature.

Hoffmeier, J. K. 2015. *The Archaeology of the Bible*. Grand Rapids MI: Kregel Publications.

Jagersma, H. 1982. *A History of Israel in the Old Testament Period*. London: SCM Press.

Levy, Th. E. (ed.). 1995. *The Archaeology of Society in the Holy Land*. Leicester: Leicester University Press.

Mazar, A. 1990. *Archaeology of the Land of the Bible, 10,000–586 BCE*. New York: Doubleday.

Moorey, P. R. S. 1991. *A Century of Biblical Archaeology*. Cambridge: Lutterworth.

Myers, E. (ed.). 1997. *The Oxford Encyclopaedia of Archaeology in the Near East*. Oxford: Oxford University Press.

Silberman, N. A. 1982. *Digging for God and Country; Explorations, Archaeology, and the Secret Struggle for the Holy Land, 1799–1917*. New York: Anchor Books/Doubleday.

Stern, E. (ed.). 1993. *New Encyclopaedia of Archaeological Excavations in the Holy Land*. Jerusalem: Carta.

Thompson, Th. L. 1999. *The Bible in History: How Writers Create a Past*. Cambridge: Pimlico. An abstract of the book written by the author is posted at: www.bibleinterp.com/articles/copenhagen.shtml.

Tuchman, B. W. 1956. *Bible and Sword: How the British came to Palestine*. New York: University of New York Press.

Van der Toorn, K. 2009. *Scribal Culture and the Making of the Hebrew Bible*. Cambridge MA: Harvard University Press.

Chapter 2

A large-scale image of the Beni Hassan tomb can be assessed at: http://upload.wikimedia.org/wikipedia/commons/thumb/f/fa/Beni-Hassan-Asiatiques2.jpg/800px-Beni-Hassan-Asiatiques2.jpg.

A part of the discussion between maximalists and minimalists is to be found at: www.bibleinterp.com/topics/Minimalism_essays.shtml.

Dever, W. 2010. *What Did the Biblical Writers Know and When Did They Know It? What Archaeology Can Tell Us About the Reality of Ancient Israel*. Grand Rapids MI: Eerdmans.

Finkelstein, I. & Silberman, N.A. 2001. *The Bible Unearthed; Archaeology's New Vision of Ancient Israel and the Origin of its Sacred Texts*. New York: Free Press.

Jagersma, H. 1992. *A History of Israel in the Old Testament Period*. London: SCM Press.

Kisilevitz, S. 2015. The Iron IIA Judahite Temple at Tel Moẓa. *Tel Aviv* 42, 147–64.

Lemche, N. P. 1991. *The Canaanites and their Land*. Sheffield: Sheffield Academic Press.

Liverani, M. 2005. *Israel's History and the History of Israel*. Sheffield: Equinox.

Redford, D. B. 1993, *Egypt, Canaan and Israel in Ancient Times*. Princeton NJ: Princeton University Press.

Thompson, Th. L. 1999. *The Bible in History: How Writers Create a Past*. Cambridge: Pimlico.

Tubb, J. 1999. *Canaanites*. Norman OK: University of Oklahoma Press.

Chapter 3

On the gods and goddesses of Canaan, see: www.metmuseum.org/toah/hd/cana/hd_cana.htm.

For Jericho see: www.bibleodyssey.org/places/main-articles/jericho.

For information on Khirbat al-Lehun: www.lehun-excavations.be.

More on the Gezer inscription at: www.kchanson.com/ANCDOCS/westsem/gezer.html.

A survey of the biblical stories on king Saul and their interpretations can be found at: www.newworldencyclopedia.org/entry/Saul.

Borowski, O. 2003. *Daily life in Biblical Times*. Atlanta GA: Society of Biblical Literature.

Killebrew, A. E. 2005. *Biblical Peoples and Ethnicity: An Archaeological Study of Egyptians, Canaanites, Philistines, and Early Israel, 1300-1100 BCE*. Atlanta GA: Society of Biblical Literature.

King, P. & Stager, L. 2002. *Life in Biblical Israel*. Louisville KE: Westminster John Knox Press.

Meyers, C. 1988. *Discovering Eve: Ancient Israelite Women in Context*. Oxford: Oxford University Press.

Pardee, D. 2002. *Ritual and Cult at Ugarit*. Atlanta GA: Society of Biblical Literature.

Smelik, K. A. D. 1992. *Writings from Ancient Israel: A Handbook of Historical and Religious Documents*. Louisville KE: Westminster John Knox Press.

Chapter 4

Information on the temple at Medinet Habu and the inscriptions is to be found at: www.bibleplaces.com/medinethabu.htm.

A photo and description of the inscription in the temple at Ekron phase 1 can be found at: www.kchanson.com/ANCDOCS/westsem/ekron.html.

The dissertation of Fred Woudhuizen, *The Ethnicity of the Sea Peoples*, can be downloaded from: www.woudhuizen.nl/fred/seapeoples.html.

Bierling, N. 1992. *Giving Goliath his due: New Archaeological Light on the Philistines*. Grand Rapids MI: Baker Book House.

Cline, E. 2015. *1177 BC: The Year Civilization Collapsed*. Princeton NJ: Princeton University Press.

Dothan, M. 1997. Tel Miqne – Ekron: an Iron Age I Philistine Settlement in Israel. In N. A. Silberman & D. B. Small, *The Archaeology of Israel; Constructing the Past, Interpretating the Present*, 96–106. London: Bloomsbury T&T Clark.

Dothan, T. & Dothan, M. 1992. *Peoples of the Sea; the Search for the Philistines*. London: Macmillan.

Ehrlich, C.S. 1996. *The Philistines in Transition; a History from ca. 1000-730 BCE*. Leiden: Brill.

Killebrew, A. E. 2005. *Biblical Peoples and Ethnicity; An Archaeological Study of Egyptians, Canaanites, Philistines, and Early Israel, 1300-1100 BCE*. Atlanta GA: Society of Biblical Literature.

Mazar, A. 2008. From 1200 to 850 BCE: Remarks on Some Selected Archaeological Issues. In L. L. Grabbe (ed.), *Israel in Transition, From Late Bronze II to Iron IIa (c. 1250-850 BCE). Volume 1. The Archaeology*, 86–120. London: Bloomsbury.

Chapter 5

The article Kings of Controversy in the National Geographic can be read at: www.nationalgeographic.com/magazine/2010/12/david-and-solomon/.

www.itsgila.com/highlightsmegiddo.htm gives the arguments used by Finkelstein and Franklin for their thesis that the 'stables' are really stables for horses. With many photographs.

Cantrell, D. 2011. *The Horseman of Israel: Horses and Chariotry in Monarchic Israel (ninth–eighth centuries BCE)*. University Park PA: Eisenbrauns.

Finkelstein, I. & Silberman, N.A. 2006. *David and Solomon: in Search of the Bible's Sacred Kings and the Roots of the Western Tradition*. New York: Simon and Schuster.

Mazar, E. 2006. Did I find King David's Palace? *Biblical Archaeology Review* 32, 16–27, 70. This article can be found at: www.biblicalarchaeology.org/daily/biblical-sites-places/jerusalem/did-i-find-king-davids-palace/.

Steiner, M. L. 2009. 'Palace of David' Reconsidered in the Light of Earlier Excavations. This review of Mazar's discoveries is published at: www.bibleinterp.com/articles/palace_2468.shtml.

Chapter 6

An extensive analysis of the battle at Qarqar is to be found at: www.livius.org/articles/battle/qarqar-853-bce/.

More on Samaria at: www.bibleodyssey.org/places/main-articles/samaria and https://biblewalks.com/sites/SamariaCity.html#AhabPalace.

Finkelstein, I. 2013. *The Forgotten Kingdom: the Archaeology and History of Northern Israel*. Atlanta GA: Society of Biblical Literature. This book is available at: www.sbl-site.org/assets/pdfs/9781589839106dwld_txt.pdf.

Franklin, N. 2008. Trademarks of the Omride Builders? In A. Fantalkin & A. Yasur-Landau (eds), *Bene Israel: Studies in the Archaeology of Israel and the Levant during the Bronze and Iron Ages in Honour of Israel Finkelstein*, 45–54. Leiden: Brill.

Korpel, M. C. A. 2008. Fit for a Queen: Jezebel's royal seal. *Biblical Aracheology Review* 32, 32–37. This article is to be found at: www.biblicalarchaeology.org/daily/biblical-artifacts/inscriptions/fit-for-a-queen-jezebels-royal-seal/.

Chapter 7

Daviau, P. M. M. & Dion, P. 2002. Moab comes to life. *Biblical Archaeology Review* 28, 38–49, 63.

Dearman, A. (ed.) 1989. *Studies in the Mesha inscription and Moab*. Riga: Scholars Press.

Lemaire, A. 1994. 'House of David' restored in ancient Moabite inscription. *Biblical Archaeology Review* 20, 30–37.

Routledge, B. 2004. *Moab in the Iron Age: Hegemony, Polity, Archaeology*. Philadelphia PA: University of Pennsylvania Press.

Smelik, K. A. D. 1992. *Writings from Ancient Israel: A Handbook of Historical and Religious Documents*. Louisville KE: Westminster John Knox Press.

Steiner, M. L. 2013. Moab during the Iron Age II Period. In M. L. Steiner & A. E. Killebrew, *The Oxford Handbook of the Archaeology of the Levant, c. 8000–332 BCE*, 770–781. Oxford: Oxford University Press.

Chapter 8

Abraham, K. 2011. The reconstruction of Jewish communities in the Persian Empire: The Al-Yahūdu clay tablets. In H. Segev (ed.), *Light and Shadows - The Catalog - The Story of Iran and the Jews*, 264–268. Tel Aviv: Beit Hatfutsot.

Faust, A. 2012, *Judah in the Neo-Babylonian Period; The Archaeology of Desolation*. Atlanta GA: Society of Biblical Literature. The Introduction to this book can be found at: www.sbl-site.org/assets/pdfs/pubs/061718P.front.pdf.

Wunsch, C. 2013. Glimpses on the lives of deportees in rural Babylonia. In A. Berlejung & M. P. Streck (eds), *Arameans, Chaldeans and Arabs in Mesopotamia and Palestine*, 247–260. Leipzig: Harrassowitz.

For the Sumerian epic 'Enmerkar and the Lord of Aratta' see Arnold, B. T. & Byer, B. E. 2002. *Readings from the Ancient Near East; Primary Sources for Old Testament Study*, 71. Ada MI: Baker Academic.

Chapter 9

The English translation of the inscription by Baruch A. Levine is to be found at: www.livius.org/sources/content/deir-alla-inscription/. He made a slightly different combination of the fragments.

Hoftijzer, J. & Van der Kooij, G. (eds), *The Balaam Text from Deir Alla Re-evaluated. Proceedings of the Symposium Held at Leiden, 21-24 August 1989*. Leiden: Brill 1991.

Smelik, K. A. D. 1992. *Writings from Ancient Israel; A Handbook of Historical and Religious Documents*. Louisville KE: Westminster John Knox Press.

Steiner, M. L. & Wagemakers, B. 2019. *Digging up the Bible? The Excavations at Tell Deir Alla, Jordan (1960-1967)*. Leiden: Sidestone Press.

Van der Kooij, G. & Ibrahim, M. M. (eds) 1989. *Picking up the Threads: a Continuing Review of Excavations at Deir Alla, Jordan*. Leiden: University of Leiden, Archaeological Centre.

Chapter 10

In Yavne, a Philistine city along the coast, hundreds of cult stands in the shape of houses or temples have been found in a repository. Look for these and many other objects at: http://www.antiquities.org.il/t/item_en.aspx?CurrentPageKey=15_1. The Yavne stands are items 15–94.

Ackerman, S. 1992. *Under Every Green Tree, Popular Religion in Sixth-Century Judah*. Riga: Scholars Press.

Becking, B. M., Dijkstra, M., Korpel, M. & Vriezen, K. 2002. *Only One God? Monotheism in Ancient Israel and the Veneration of the Goddess Asherah*. Sheffield: Sheffield Academic Press.

Darby, E. D. 2014. *Interpreting Judean Pillar Figurines; Gender and Empire in Judean Apotropaic Ritual*. Heidelberg: Mohr Siebeck.

Darby, E. D. 2015. Fatal attraction: obsession, aversion, and the femme fatale of ancient Judah. www.bibleinterp.com/articles/2015/02/dar398024.shtml.

Dever, W. 2005. *Did God have a Wife? Archaeology and Folk Religion in Ancient Israel*. Grand Rapids MI: Eerdmans Press.

Hadley, J. 2000. *The Cult of Asherah in Ancient Israel and Judah: Evidence for a Hebrew Goddess*. Cambridge: Cambridge University Press. A review of this book can be found at: http://sites.utoronto.ca/wjudaism/journal/spring2002/documents/hadley.pdf. For more 'Evidence on Asherah' see J. Hadley's article of the same name at: http://www.bibleinterp.com/articles/ashart1212.shtml.

Korpel, M. C. A. 2002. Asherah outside Israel. In B. Becking *et al.* 2002, 127–50.

Mazar, A. & Cohen-Panitz, N. 2008. To what God? Altars and a house shrine from Tel Rehov Puzzle archaeologists. *Biblical Archaeology Review* 2008, 40–7. The article that Z. Meshel wrote shortly after the excavations of Kuntillet Ajrud is to be found at: www.penn.museum/documents/publications/expedition/pdfs/20-4/meshel.pdf.

Patai, R. 1990. *The Hebrew Goddess*. 3rd enlarged edition. Detroit MI: Wayne State University Press.

Stone, M. 1978. *When God was a woman*. New York: Mariner Books.

Zevit, A. 2001. *The Religions of Ancient Israel: A Synthesis of Parallactic Approaches*. New York: Continuum. A review can be found at: www.jhsonline.org/reviews/review032.htm.

Chapter 11

An extensive website deals with the problem of the location of Jerusalem's temple: www.templemount.org.

(Much) more on Flavius Josephus can be found at: www.livius.org.

Images and a short description of the temple of Arad are at: https://www.bibleplaces.com/arad/.

Extensive descriptions of Samaria and the temple at: https://www.livius.org/articles/place/samaria/.

For those interested in the excavations at Mount Gerizim: https://biblewalks.com/sites/mountGerizim.html.

On the website www.bibleinterp.com you can find critical articles on the fake inscriptions and the official reports of the research committees.

Gibson, S. & Jacobson, D. M. 1996. *Below the Temple Mount in Jerusalem: a Sourcebook on the Cisterns, Subterranean Chambers and Conduits of the Haram al-Sharif*. Oxford: British Archaeological Report S637.

Goldhill, S. 2005. *The Temple of Jerusalem*. Cambrdige MA: Harvard University Press.

Grabar, O. & Kedar, B. Z. (eds). 2010. *Where Heaven and Earth Meet. Jerusalem's Sacred Esplanade*. Austin TX: University of Texas Press. A book on the Temple Mount, written by a Jew, a Christian and a Muslim (who disagree on more or less everything).

Jagersma, H. 1994. *A History of Israel from Alexander the Great to Bar Kochba*. London: SCM Press.

Flavius Josephus. *The Jewish War*. There are many English translations.

Ritmeyer, L. & Ritmeyer, K. 1998. *Secrets of Jerusalem's Temple Mount*. Washington DC: Biblical Archaeology Society. Leen Ritmeyer is an architect who has drawn many reconstructions of ancient buildings. Check out his website: www.ritmeyer.com.

Shanks, H. 2007. *Jerusalem's Temple Mount: From Solomon to the Golden Dome*. New York: Continuum.

Porten, B. 1996. *The Elephantine Papyri in English; Three Millennia of Cross-Cultural Continuity and Change*. Leiden: Brill.